Defending Latina/o
Immigrant Communities

Defending Latina/o Immigrant Communities

The Xenophobic Era of Trump and Beyond

Alvaro Huerta

Hamilton Books

Lanham • Boulder • New York • Toronto • London

Published by Hamilton Books
An imprint of The Rowman & Littlefield Publishing Group, Inc.
4501 Forbes Boulevard, Suite 200, Lanham, Maryland 20706
Hamilton Books Acquisitions Department (301) 459-3366

6 Tinworth Street, London SE11 5AL

British Library Cataloguing in Publication Information Available

Library of Congress Control Number: 2019941423

ISBN 978-0-7618-7127-9 (pbk. : alk. paper)
ISBN 978-0-7618-7128-6 (electronic)

∞™ The paper used in this publication meets the minimum requirements of American National Standard for Information Sciences Permanence of Paper for Printed Library Materials, ANSI/NISO Z39.48-1992.

Dedications

This book is dedicated to all of the people who've had a positive impact on my life. With all of my accomplishments—e.g., overcoming abject poverty and violence, securing university-based and community organizing victories, earning advanced degrees and academic positions, publishing journal articles and books, conducting lectures and TEDx talks, etc.— I've been in a privileged position to advocate on behalf of Latinas/os in general and Mexicans on both sides of *la frontera* in particular—my clan.

For me, everything starts and ends with the Mexican people and those who believe in imagining a better world.

This includes my friends (especially childhood friends from the Ramona Gardens housing project or Big Hazard projects), fellow organizers, and colleagues.

This mostly includes my extended Mexican family: parents (Carmen, Salomon), siblings (Catalina, Soledad, Ofelia, Salomon, Rosa, Noel, and Ismael), grandparents, nephews, nieces, uncles, aunts, in-laws, and cousins—my first cousins are more like siblings.

In a time when my family experienced a great loss with the passing of my brother Noel (or Nene), it has been a very difficult period for us. No amount of individual (or group) success will bring us the same joy that Noel brought us. We will always love you and never forget you, Nene!

I especially dedicate this book to my wise and beautiful wife, Antonia. She constantly encourages me to pursue my academic goals, civic engagement actions and public policy objectives. Her life-long leadership as an educator and a social justice advocate motivates me to get ahead.

Finally, Antonia and I dedicate this book to our amazing and brilliant son, Joaquin. His wit, compassion for others, loyalty to his friends, pride of Mexican heritage, and love for family inspires us daily.

In Memoriam

Noel "Nene" Huerta (1971–2017)
Carmen Mejia Huerta (1939–2011)
Salomon Chavez Huerta (1930–1996)
Librada Montes (1938–2018)
Roberto Montes (1921–2012)

"Anti-Mexicanism is a form of nativism practiced by colonialists and their inheritors."
—Dr. Juan Gómez-Quiñones (2019)

Contents

List of Figures

Foreword

Dr. José Z. Calderón

This book is a monograph of various articles that focus on the systemic issues of inequality, racism, and exclusion aimed primarily at Latino and Latina immigrant communities. Also, it centers on the forms of organizing, networks, and coalition models that are emerging to overcome this historical oppression. With the changing demographics, where Latinos and Latinas are now the largest minority group in the U.S. and rapidly becoming a majority group in various U.S. cities, there is a need for a publication that identifies the role that Latino and Latina immigrants play in these transformations.

Dr. Alvaro Huerta, a joint-faculty member in the Departments of Urban & Regional Planning and Ethnic & Women's Studies at California State Polytechnic University, Pomona, is highly productive in writing books and articles on these issues. He has made a name for himself through publishing in such important publication periodicals such as the *Los Angeles Business Journal*, *The Progressive,* and the *Huffington Post*.

Some of his articles, included here, on Mexican immigrants and their networks in the informal economy flow from a passion rooted in his experiences of growing up in an immigrant family with a working-class father—as a farmworker, factory janitor, and day laborer. Like his father, various articles in this monograph present the reality of most Latina/o immigrant families coming to the U.S., as a result of years of this country's foreign policies toward those countries and a fomenting of violence and poverty. These reasons have included the economic inequalities that exist between the U.S. and Latin America by the uprooting of farmers and peasants as a result of trade agreements, such as NAFTA. These unequal trade agreements favor the subsidized multinational corporate interests in this country, resulting in the undercutting of staple crops in the sending countries, such as beans and corn.

In addition to analyzing what a poor job the media and politicians have done in bringing out the real reasons for this migration, Huerta also criticizes city leaders, old-school urban planners, and architects in his field for exclusionary planning policies. These policies advance a distorted view and reality of the many contributions that immigrants make to this country. Moreover, we have seen the rise of a rabid racism and nativism promoted by the likes of President Donald J. Trump with cries that our immigrant brothers and sisters have no right to be here and should be immediately deported.

Huerta presents solid arguments in defending immigrant families for their contributions that amount to hundreds of billions of dollars to the U.S. economy through their labor power, purchasing power, businesses and taxes. In addition to criticizing Republicans for their anti-immigrant policies—that he predicts they will one day regret—Huerta does not hold back in criticizing the former-President Barack Obama's administration for carrying out the largest deportations of immigrants (at 2.7 million) of any president in recent history.

In proposing alternative strategies, Huerta analyzes the rise of grass-roots social movements that focus on the needs for investment in quality housing, education, employment, and health. In looking to the future, Huerta looks at alternative organizing strategies for sustaining a movement that thwarts the criminalization of our immigrant communities to advance policies that lead to legalization, permanent residency, and citizenship with no expansion of temporary guest worker programs and with labor law protections.

On a personal level, I share many similarities with Huerta and the honest, hard-working people he writes about in this insightful and important book. While I was born in Mexico, I was raised in the U.S. under harsh economic realities. Being the first in my family to pursue higher education, like Huerta, I started my activism during my undergraduate studies. Learning about my history or the fact that my history had been ignored or relegated to second-class status in mainstream education, I then spent many years as a community organizer.

As a community organizer during the early stages of the Chicana/o movement, I committed my life to advocating for those on the margins. This included working on behalf of the farmworkers with the United Farm Workers (UFW). After spending many years defending the rights of immigrants, the poor, and racialized communities, I pursued my doctoral studies at UCLA. This is when I first met Huerta, while teaching an undergraduate course that he enrolled in. At the time, Huerta was highly involved in MEChA (*Movimiento Estudiantil Chicana/o de Aztlán*), as a student activist, and, later, like myself, as a community organizer.

Many years later, our paths have crossed again, as scholar-activists. Having both the theory and practice of social movements on our side, it only makes sense that I write this foreword for my colleague, collaborator, good friend, and fellow agitator in these turbulent and dark times.

Introduction

Dr. Alvaro Huerta

As a social scientist, public intellectual and former community activist, I wrote these short essays and stories—from 2008 to 2019—in defense of one of the most vilified, demonized and vulnerable groups in the United States: Latina/o immigrants. While some of these essays are written in the past tense, others are written in the present tense, responding to ongoing racist rhetoric and xenophobic policies against brown people by American leaders (mostly conservative), media outlets (e.g., Fox News) and millions of average citizens.

In a time when many people, especially the youth, are preoccupied or bombarded with social media outlets, video games and mobile devices, etc., too often, it becomes challenging for them to keep up with important current affairs (and historical events) which negatively impact immigrants, racialized communities and the working-class in this country. Thus, to compete for their attention, when discussing and debating important matters (domestic and international), I strongly believe that the short essay (and short story)—when written in a clear and an accessible language—represents an effective means of communication for scholars, policy makers, journalists, community activists and others who defend and advocate for historically marginalized communities.

While I'm trained as an interdisciplinary scholar with both quantitative and qualitative research skills and experience—where I conduct research and publish in traditional academic venues, such as peer-reviewed journals and university presses—in the tradition of Native Americans, I also believe in the power of storytelling, as part of my long-time efforts to defend and humanize immigrants. In other words, it's not enough to say that there are millions of productive immigrants in the workforce or millions of vulnerable immigrants without legal status supported by sophisticated statistics, charts and tables with the aim to educate and influence the American leaders, policy makers and public (or a segment of it) to build an equitable and just society. While stats, charts and tables are important in conducting research studies on vulnerable groups, it's also imperative for those of us who care about equality and justice to share real stories of Latina/o immigrants (and their offspring), as human beings, with dreams and aspirations for a better life not only for themselves, but also for their families. In this context, by including stories of my large Mexican family in *el norte*, I seek to shed light on one particular case, like millions of other untold stories about oppressed groups, to provide more nuanced narratives and perspectives of people of Mexican heritage in this country. This includes stories of struggle, sacrifice, resilience, advancement, generosity, love and loss.

Moreover, while this book serves as a text (historical and contemporary) against draconian immigration policies in this country, it also serves as an example of how scholars and others (e.g., politicians, policy makers, journalists, teachers, union leaders, non-profit leaders) should respond to the inhumane and unjust policies against Latina/o immigrants, racialized groups and the working-class in this country.

While I primarily focus on key issues impacting Latina/o immigrants, I also discuss issues related to race, class, place and state violence. For this book, I relied on my rigorous scholarly training, public policy knowledge and community activist background. As a son of Mexican immigrants, my personal and familial experiences also informed this book with the aim of defending and humanizing *los de abajo*/those on the bottom.

In terms of the book's contents, in addition to Dr. José Z. Calderón's excellent foreword, it includes two outstanding essays by Dr. Juan Gómez-Quiñones—an acclaimed scholar and activist, like Dr. Calderón. Dr. Gómez-Quiñones' essay on anti-Mexicanism represents a groundbreaking paradigm and enormous contribution to the fields of Chicana/o Studies and American Studies. His other insightful essay centers on the police killing of the journalist Ruben Salazar (and others deaths) during the Chicana/o Moratorium protest in East Los Angeles on August 29, 1970. There's also an important essay on street vendors by contributing author Joaquin Montes Huerta—a young scholar, college student and emerging leader.

Like my first book, *Reframing the Latino Immigration Debate: Towards a Humanistic Paradigm*, this book incorporates excellent photos of established photographers, along with family photos. The established photographers include Ed Carreón and Pablo Aguilar, representing positive role models for current and future photographers, particularly Latinas/os. Also, it includes a superb illustration of Andrew Huerta—an accomplished comic artist. Coincidentally, Andrew, who continues to expand the scope of his art, happens to be my nephew.

This book also includes the brilliant art of Salomon Huerta—an internationally acclaimed artist. As a collaborator, Salomon (my brother) also contributed the amazing cover art for this book. Given that Salomon has gained more than his fair share of 15 minutes of fame that the legendary artist Andy Warhol promised all of us will get in the future, but only a few ever obtain, I'm proud that my brother and I could combine our skills and efforts to produce this book. (On second thought, maybe I just asked him to collaborate with me to sell more books? If I did so, I hope nobody tells him!)

While I don't suffer from imposter syndrome or any other syndrome, given my bleak upbringing in an impoverished Mexican *colonia* and a violent American barrio, growing up, I never imagined or dreamed of being a published author or becoming a scholar. In fact, while I was above average in mathematics throughout my childhood and teenage years, when it came to reading and writing, I was below average. Instead of blaming myself for not reading and writing at grade level—which I originally did—I now blame the poor and inadequate K–12 education that I received in America's inner-city public schools. (It doesn't help when you're only assigned one book to read, *The Pearl* by John Steinbeck, and one 2-page paper, double-spaced, to write throughout your entire K–12 education!)

It wasn't until the end of my sophomore year at UCLA (where I originally majored in mathematics) when I decided to teach myself how to read and write (at the university level) in order to compete with my peers, where I transformed my academic and professional trajectory for the better. This provides some context for the birth of this book (my third) and forthcoming ones (for major university presses) that I'm diligently working on.

Thus, by writing from an insider-outsider positionality—personally, an integral member of an immigrant family and, professionally, far removed from it—this book aims to counter the pejorative portrayals of Latina/o immigrants in the U.S. It also seeks to re-frame how Latina/o immigrants—as people on the move—should be viewed and treated with dignity and respect.

ONE

Brief History Notes on Mexican Immigration to the U.S.

Dr. Alvaro Huerta

The historical ties of Mexican immigrants to the U.S., specifically the Southwest, distinguishes people of Mexican origin from other immigrant groups, especially those from Europe. While Mexican immigrants continue to be demonized and characterized as "criminals," "drug dealers," "rapists," "illegal aliens" and "invaders" by American leaders and millions of white citizens, they have essentially become "foreigners in their own land."

In his infamous article, "The Hispanic Threat," (*Foreign Policy*, 2009), the late Dr. Samuel P. Huntington of Harvard claimed that Latinas/os in general and individuals of Mexican origin in particular represented an existential threat to the U.S. By evaluating the positive contributions of Latinas/os to this country since the mid-1800s, we can easily dismiss racist labels and false narratives by small-minded American leaders, racist scholars and nativist citizens. Moreover, by being objective and critical, we can learn the true history about the actual invaders. For instance, in progressive history books, like Dr. Ronald Takaki's *A Different Mirror: A History of Multicultural America*, we learn that white Americans gradually migrated into what is now known as Texas during the 1820s (156).

While the Mexican government allowed for whites to settle in this foreign territory, the authorities did so under the assumption that they adopt Mexican customs, learn Spanish and intermarry with the native population. This originally occurred without too much conflict, which reveals the openness of the Mexican government and its people toward the white foreigners. This is not to imply that all whites arrived legally or with permission from the Mexican government, as Gloria Anzaldúa eloquently documents in her 1987 classic book, *Borderland/La Frontera: The New Mestiza*.

By 1826, according to Takaki, then-President John Quincy Adams offered the Mexican government $1 million for Texas, where the Mexican government refused (156). Once Mexico outlawed slavery in 1830, pro-slavery Americans, along with other white settlers, rebelled and formed The Republic of Texas in 1836. By 1845, it was annexed into the United States. It appears to me that the white settlers or *gringos* took the Mexicans literally when the hosts generously said, *"Mi casa es su casa."*

Once the U.S. government annexed Texas, it didn't take the government long to pursue additional territory via the U.S. imperialist war against Mexico (1846 to 1848), as documented by Chicana/o historians, such as Dr. Juan Gómez-Quiñones, Dr. Deena J. González and Dr. Rudolfo "Rudy" Acuña. Based on Manifest Destiny, this imperialist war represented a bloody and greedy land grab, where, according to Acuña in his classic book, *Occupied America: A History of Chicanos*, this concept represents ". . . a religious doctrine with roots in Puritan ideas, which continue to influence U.S. thought to this day" (52). After the U.S. forced Mexico to sign the Treaty of Guadalupe Hidalgo on February 2, 1848, by then, Mexico lost half of its territory, according to Anzaldúa (7). Although the Mexicans who decided to reside in the U.S. were protected under the treaty, which included their ancestral lands, the U.S. Congress quickly ratified the treaty.

As a result, the Mexicans in *el norte* eventually lost their lands through the courts, illegal acts and violent means by the state and white citizens. Writing about the brutal experiences of the disposed Mexicans on this side of the border, Anzaldúa (1987) decries this tragedy: *"Con el destierro y el exilo fuimos desu ñados, destroncados, destripados*—we were jerked out by our roots, truncated, disemboweled, dispossessed, and separated from our identity and our history. Many, under the threat of Anglo terrorism, abandoned their homes and ranches and went to Mexico" (7–8). This cruel history, unfortunately, is not taught in American schools.

Thus, when we think about Mexican immigration to *el norte*, we must examine it under this historical context. That is, unlike the millions of European immigrants who travelled across an entire ocean to settle in North America, Mexicans have always occupied this land or called it home until it was stolen from them by military force. Moreover, like in the case of Native Americans and the brutal history of broken treaties by the U.S. government, the Mexicans in *el norte* lost their basic rights due to the broken Treaty of Guadalupe Hidalgo. Given their historical memory, this is one reason why the millions of Mexicans who make their journey to the U.S. (with or without legal status), especially to the Southwest, don't view themselves as law breakers or so-called "illegals."

Like the homing pigeon, the Mexican is returning to the motherland.

Despite the loss of their ancestral lands, the impact or contributions of Mexicans (immigrants, residents and citizens) to American cities, suburbs, rural communities and agricultural fields during the past 170 years has been positive, overall. Moreover, while Mexicans in *el norte* don't receive the credit that they deserve, they've contributed greatly (and continue to the present) in many areas of American society and its economy. This includes agriculture, music, art, construction, infrastructure, transportation (e.g., railroads, freeways, roads), medicine, mining, ranching, science, the military, the academy and beyond. Essentially, there's no doubt that individuals of Mexican origin played a key role (to the present) to help make this country become the richest, most advanced and powerful country in the world.

Despite being defeated militarily during the early and mid-1800s and experiencing institutional racism, Mexicans have migrated to this country—along with those who've settled prior to the U.S. imperialist war against Mexico—to work, create jobs, study, serve in the military and raise families, etc. For instance, during the second half of the 1800s, Mexican immigrants and their offspring represented a key labor force in agriculture, railroad construction, mining and other key sectors. However, instead of being rewarded for their labor contributions with adequate financial compensation and upward mobility opportunities, they've experienced racism (to the present) in the workforce and beyond. According to Takaki, working on white-owned ranches in Texas, "Mexican laborer[s] found themselves in a caste system — a racially stratified occupational hierarchy" (173).

During most of the 1800s and 1900s, it was very common to see Mexicans and Chicanas/os (Mexican-Americans) employed as laborers or workers, while whites worked as supervisors or managers. This racial hierarchy in the workforce, along with the unequal educational system, has limited the occupational status of Mexican immigrants and Chicanas/os. For instance, Mexican immigrants were relegated to the bottom of the economic workforce, which included toiling under agricultural programs like the Bracero Program—the U.S.-Mexico guest worker program of the mid-twentieth century. From 1942 to 1964, more than 4.8 million Mexican immigrants legally migrated to this country, representing "cheap," exploitable labor for agricultural employers for the benefit of American consumers (Gonzales 175). Many of them also worked to build America's railroad infrastructure.

Despite being conquered and exploited in the workforce, the Mexican people in *el norte* have a strong tradition of organizing for social and economic justice. According to Takaki, in 1903, ". . . hundreds of Mexicans and Japanese farm workers went on strike in Oxnard, California" (174). This is just one example, apart from the case of the United Farm Workers (UFW) and Brown Berets of the 1960s and 1970s, where Mexicans and Chicanas/os defended their labor and civil rights through labor strikes, civil disobedience, protests, marches and so on.

Moreover, despite being a racialized minority in this country, Mexicans and Chicanas/os served in the military at higher rates compared to whites. According to Acuña, where he cites Robin Scott, during WWII, while Chicanas/os represented only 2.69 million residents/citizens in the U.S., between 375,000 to 500,000 Chicanos served in the war (243). Despite their contributions and sacrifices, it didn't stop the U.S. government from implementing "Operation Wetback" in early 1954, where Mexican immigrants and Chicanas/os were deported in mass to Mexico. It's obvious to me that the military and labor contributions of Chicanas/os, like in the present, weren't appreciated by the U.S. government.

As a son of Mexican immigrants, this issue is not just an academic exercise for me; it's also personal. Like millions of her *paisanas*, while my late mother Carmen toiled in the informal economy as a domestic worker in this country for many decades, privileged whites pursued economic opportunities and leisure activities outside of the household. Similarly, like millions of his *paisanos*, while my late father Salomon first arrived in this country to pick fruits and vegetables during the Bracero Program, where he was forced to abandon his family and rural community, American families enjoyed the fruits of his labor in their homes and restaurants.

At the end of the day, my late parents never received the adequate financial rewards or benefits of their labor and sacrifice, such as good wages, upward mobility opportunities, educational opportunities and homeownership.

In my expert opinion, based on my interdisciplinary scholarship, civic engagement experience and public policy background, it will take many generations to come for millions of Mexicans and Chicanas/os in *el norte* to one day obtain the elusive American Dream.

TWO

La Realidad

The Realities of Anti-Mexicanism—A Paradigm

Dr. Juan Gómez-Quiñones

U.S. anti-Mexicanism is a race premised set of historical and contemporary ascriptions, convictions and discriminatory practices inflicted on persons of Mexican descent, longstanding and pervasive in the United States. This essay conceptualizes, historicizes, and analyzes anti-Mexicanism, past and present, concurrent with some references to sources. Here, the emphasis is conceptual, not historiographical. Anti-Mexicanism is a form of nativism practiced by colonialists and their inheritors. Mexicans, being natives, became targets of aggressive practices inclusive of the violence directed at Indigenous and African peoples. The words "Mexican" and "Mexico" speak to Indigenous heritages. The origins of the thought and meaning of "Mexican" and "Mexico" speak to historical native roots. White supremacist ideologues have understood this. When anti-Mexican rhetoric is used by white supremacists, those who proclaim rights to rulership, the public resonating response—violence and micro-aggressions—indicates the presence of this phenomenon.

This anti-Mexicanism practice is beyond crude prejudice or uncivil, ethnocentric chauvinism. To be sure, for some articulators, anti-Mexican words are such expressions. When anti-Mexicanism is articulated as a publically broadcasted set of negative evaluations that target Mexicans, recommends actions, and used as a means to a set of political goals, it is an ideology. Through broadcast, this ideology is validated as such by a collectivity of endorsers and enactors. This broadcasting does not parse its targeting—it is inclusive—women and men, gay and straight, disabled

9

and able bodied—all of Mexican origin are encompassed. To be sure, the deep concern in this analysis is about the future, not the past. It aims to free the children of future generations from deeply hurtful practices and a set of imagined, negative denominators impacting their self-conscious-ness and personal freedom.

The large majority of people during the evolution to what became Mexicans and Mexico were and are Indigenous and of Indigenous de-scent. Antipathy toward Native Americans is incremental upon English-speaking colonialists' arrival. Their actions generate the initial steps lead-ing to racists and white supremacy practiced in what came to be the United States. Disrespecting Indians politically is a step toward white supremacism and the eventual subordinating of Mexicans.

The hostility of European, English-speaking whites to Native Americans begins with the European arrival in what is now Groton in New London County, Connecticut. In 1637, over seven hundred Pequot men, women and children were attacked by white "colonists," as the Pequot celebrated their annual Green Corn Dance. Those who were not shot were burned alive in their ceremonial space. The next day, the then-Governor of Massachusetts declared a day of "Thanksgiving." This real episode is documented in the *Holland Documents* and the 13th volume of *Colonial Documentary History*. It's also found in the private papers of Sir William Johnson, Royal British Agent of the Colony [of New York], circa 1640s. The core of this and other contentions is land possession or territo-rial dominance.

Under European, Spanish-speaking colonialism—primarily of Indige-nous origin, with African, and European intersections—a hybrid demo-graphic becoming a "Spanish-speaking" group in Mesoamerica was an evolution toward Mexicanos, the social, and Mexicanidad, the identity. Let it be understood, this social evolution is complicated with contradic-tions aplenty, initially related to its multiple ethnic decendencies and its diverse social-economic circumstances. Even as a partial contestatory re-sponse to the colonial experience, the social evolution entails the germs and evidences, the pathologies of the colonial—including racisms, au-thoritarianisms, and elitisms.

In the anglophone sphere, among the literate, perception of Natives is affected by the so-called colonialistic "Black Legend," whereby Spanish colonialism is decried and English colonialism, by contrast, is upheld. This "legend" is a prejudiced and concocted propaganda. This dialogue deteriorates into an "Anglo-Hispanic" exchange of negatives—Protes-tantism versus Catholicism; Shakespeare versus Shakespeare. The "leg-end" could be judged as a colonialist distraction promoted by elite serv-ing intellectuals of both England and Spain who, watchful of another's colonialist methods, ignores the racist and supremacist consequences of their own colonialism over Natives and Africans and their treatment of the descendants of both groups. Thus, racism is reduced as a mere by-product of inevitable colonial technologies, when in fact the racialization of Native Americans is a central premise of European colonialism and one corollary to the subordination of Africans.

More specifically, the deep historical record of anti-Mexicanism at its basis is a result of the domination of Indians and enslavement of Blacks. This includes the North American invasion by English whites in their perennial quest for wealth, status, and power at the expense of others. A multi-faceted white supremacism arises as the rationalization to secure these wants. One can start with whites arriving in Massachusetts and Blacks in Virginia, and early persecutions of Native Americans any-where. Overtime, Indio, Africans, Afro-Mestizos and Indio-Mestizo Spanish-speakers joined the ranks of those subordinated by English colo-nialists. Indians and Africans are the human resources for the empower-ment of white colonialists, according to seventeenth and nineteenth cen-tury conditions and terms, empowering the colonialists' maintenance of power over territories and localities.

The historical record of U.S.-Mexico relations is a narrative of subordi-nation justified on racist and supremacist premises. To be sure, these are multifaceted and changing and not necessarily representationally inclu-sive of all whites. However, in fact, the record indicates U.S. citizens as the aggressors in the relation, not Mexicans. U.S. citizens are the perpe-trators of negative views, invidious-distinctions and the domineering ac-tions, according with these views.

In contrast to U.S. negativity, Mexico—as a state and economy—has been useful to U.S. ambitions, where Mexican people have been service-able to U.S. needs. Rather than respect, there are argued explicit reasons by U.S. whites from early and later negative characterizations of Indio-Mulatto-Mestizos related to whites' quest for wealth, status, and power within the aegis of their culture and values. In sum, specifically, they take from Mexico's land, resources and labor by whatever means are viable. The social views and territorial ambitions of then-President Thomas Jef-ferson, a Southern slaver, are early expressions of these wants which for long were related to benefits first derived from slaves and later racialized disempowered laborers summed in the observation: "the desire for pos-session is a disease with them." There is a historical and ideological con-text to this quest.

In many studies, "race" applies when ethnicity is judged unchange-able and so is the assigning of place in the hierarchical order of a general society co-inhabited by supra-ordinates and subordinates. These judg-ments or claims are academic myths. Racism is more complex, more fluid and perennial. For Mexicans in the United States, their mixed heritages of Native American concurrent with those heritages from Africa or Asia and some occasional European descendancy, intertwine the ethnic and racial. Among and between these of formative importance are Native American and Mexican American relations. These all encounter the age-old racial perceptions of Euro-Americans and their racialized practices. For Mexicans, thus, the social science truism applies—race is not real, but racism is—and the pressing concern is white supremacism.

Hierarchy and even ethnicity are indeed subject to change. A happenstance is that some, or many, of the oppressor and oppressed hold (and held) "racialist" *notions* of themselves, as well as the "other," whether near or across the globe. Their worldviews are racialized and this should change sometime in the future, hopefully through concerted actions.

White supremacism is a further question. Supremacism can be changed through counter empowerment actions as the micro and macro elements of the paradigm of white supremacism pinpoint. Yet, supremacism remains.

The practice of a particular social consciousness can be quite mobile and practical in the pursuits of chosen ends. Analysis of white supremacy requires interpretive elasticity and decisively diverse counter measures to encourage progressive change. One hindrance to this end, a major obstacle, is that whites have been saturated with false history(ies) of themselves; a history which supposedly has been made possible through the practices of white supremacism. Moreover, it's the fact that this false history and avowed utilitarianist, white supremacism are but two heads of a multi-head monster—a living, breathing real Hydra, an overarching hegemonic, and structured system that requires integral changes.

The U.S. Mexican "ethnic" is visualized as being socially within a historical collectivity descended from a common set of mainly native ancestors. *Consciousness* of these living legacies is formatively important, as one source of inner strength to counter anti-Mexicanism. True, the perception of outsiders bearing on this is important, but the struggle is also formidably internal. Particularly important is the extent that these influence the self-consciousness of young and adolescent Mexicans. Indeed, the consciousness of Mexicans needs change. In any case, Mexicans evolve socially, as does their collective consciousness.

Most U.S. Mexicans understand social change intuitively and counter instructively. Mexicans are likely to have some awareness of family social changes in relation to family culture and descendancy, more so than Euro-Americans who resist change—even though, as stated in any case—they also undergo changes. A revised, enriched, shared, Mexican political critical awareness can be an asset in thinking and actions to bring about positive changes. The positive and the negative need to and can be sorted out. Consciousness is an important step to counter oppression. However much complicated, the literature, concepts, and application of the terms race, racism and racialism, the cutting blade is that these are empowered through and by white supremacism beliefs and practices.

Mexican Americans are a bottom ethnic group and unless there are changes, Mexicans will remain so, even in a multi-ethnic and pluralist society, including white Latinas/os. This may be the case even if the United States becomes a significantly demographically, non-white society. This is a consequence, in part, to the diffusion of anti-Mexicanism to all sectors of U.S. society. It is not only taught to whites. Tragically, Mexicans also consume anti-Mexican propaganda and, in turn, produce and diffuse it consciously or unconsciously.

Thus, anti-Mexicanism must be challenged for the sake of the future; not the past. It must be challenged for a society in which children will be safe from past crimes.

NOTE

This essay was originally published in the HuffPost.

THREE

Immigration Should be a Basic Human Right

Dr. Alvaro Huerta

Throughout history, human beings have been in constant movement. If migration is certain and constant, why do so many Americans and their leaders make a big fuss about the migration of Latinas/os to the United States?

I will never forget the stories that my late father told me about his experiences working as part of the Bracero Program—the U.S.-Mexico guest worker program during the mid-twenieth century. While he told me about the inhumane working conditions he experienced, he held back in the details about the humiliating practices and racist acts he experienced by American government officials, labor contractors and agricultural employers. I guess he lived with the shame of not being treated like a man in silence. While living in overcrowded housing, he was also charged for food and rent from the company store. Thus, when U.S. politicians, leaders and citizens insult immigrants, they also insult the memory of my father and the millions of migrants who toiled (to the present) in our agricultural fields to produce our food.

My late mother worked as a domestic worker in this country, cleaning homes and raising children of privileged Americans. She treated these children like her own. I can still remember when my mother cried when the blond, blue-eyed kid she was caring for left to Chicago when the family relocated. I recall joking with her about the fact that she didn't cry when I moved out of the house at seventeen years of age to attend UCLA. While not too far in distance, for a Chicano teen from public housing projects, moving from East Los Angeles to West Los Angeles was like moving from California to Chicago!

My older sisters also worked as domestic workers in this country, starting as young as thirteen years old. We all benefit from immigrant workers!

In her research and lectures, Dr. Bridget Anderson of Oxford University contends that we should strive for a world without borders. While some call her views utopian, she counters that borders are a dystopia. Moreover, Dr. Michael Dear of UC Berkeley, as Professor Emeritus, argues a similar point in his insightful book, *Why Walls Won't Work: Repairing the U.S.-Mexico Divide*, about the failure of border walls. By analyzing history, he predicts that all border walls will eventually come down.

We all start in one place and end up in another. Most Americans leave home for better jobs, education or simply for love. Aspiring immigrants should have the right to fulfill their dreams and aspirations.

In short, freedom to migrate should be a basic human right.

DEATH, TAXES AND MIGRATION

In life, as the saying goes, nothing is certain except for death and taxes. I propose another: migration. Migration represents a universal human right. While some economists want us to believe that humans migrate, especially the global poor, to more developed countries for better jobs and higher wages, throughout history, humans have also migrated because of climate change, natural disaster, disease, violence, war, repression, dictatorships, religious persecution, drug wars, gang warfare, free trade agreements and global capitalism.

Humans have been in constant movement and always will be. If migration is certain and constant, why do so many Americans and their leaders, particularly conservatives, fuss about Latina/o immigration to the United States?

As a scholar and public policy expert, I'm interested on immigration-related issues and other wicked problems, domestically and internationally, as I constantly seek to understand the complex nature of immigration. When American leaders label immigrants "illegal aliens," "anchor babies" and "threats to national security," the greater society will have less sympathy for these human beings, especially when they're exploited in the workforce or deported and separated from their families.

Instead of attacking and objectifying immigrants, let's appreciate their humanity and positive contributions to society. I will never forget the stories my late Mexican father, Salomon Chavez Huerta, told me about his experiences during the Bracero Program—the U.S.-Mexico guest worker program of the mid-twentieth century. As he, along with his *paisanos*, toiled in this country's agricultural fields for meager wages, they were treated like beasts of burden.

Once my father's agricultural contract expired, my family moved from his small *rancho* in the beautiful Mexican state of Michoacán to the border city of Tijuana, Baja California. Once settled in Tijuana, my late mother, Carmen Mejia Huerta, worked as a trans-border domestic worker in San Diego, California. She worked under a work visa. Apart from cleaning homes for privileged Americans, she treated the children she cared for like her own. And for this, what did my mother receive? Poor wages, lack of work benefits and disrespect.

During one of her extended work stays in the U.S., while pregnant with me, my mother, as a rational actor, decided that I was going to be born in this country. Thus, with the help of extended family members in northern California, I was born in Sacramento. This is exactly how migrant networks function.

Forty days after my birth, I was united with my siblings and extended family in Tijuana, where I spent the first four years of my life. My parents eventually migrated to *el norte*, where we lived in Hollywood for a couple of years prior to moving to East Los Angeles' notorious Ramona Gardens housing project. This housing project is better known for its dominant gang: the Big Hazard projects. During the time that I was growing up in the projects, especially during the late 1970s and mid-1980s (and beyond), it represented one of the most dangerous barrios in the country.

While my father worked as janitor, my mother worked as a domestic worker in West Los Angeles. Thanks to their hard work, four of their eight children attended elite universities: UCLA, UC Berkeley, UCSB and Art Center College of Design in Pasadena.

Prior to becoming an academic, I earned my PhD in City and Regional Planning from UC Berkeley. I also earned my BA in History and MA in Urban Planning from UCLA. My wife Antonia, as a daughter of Mexican immigrants, also graduated from UCLA, where we met. Our Mexican immigrant parents sacrificed their bodies and dreams so we could have opportunities not available to them in their home country.

We all benefit from immigrant labor, provided by millions of people, like my late Mexican parents and in-laws. So why are Americans so fixated with borders? Can we imagine a world without borders? In her amazing TEDx talk, Dr. Bridget Anderson of Oxford University argues in the affirmative, where we should strive for this idea to become a reality. Similarly, should we—those of us who envision a more just world—demand that American leaders tear down our southern border?

Before people judge and denigrate immigrants, they must ask themselves some basic questions. For example, did their ancestors ever migrate? Do they still live in the neighborhood where they were born or raised? Have they ever migrated or plan to do so?

FOUR

The Day I Learned
I was Poor and Mexican

Dr. Alvaro Huerta

When you grow up in a poor, segregated community, often times, you're oblivious of your class status and ethnicity. Growing up in tight-knit Mexican communities, from Tijuana in Mexico to East Los Angeles in the U.S., I didn't realize that I was poor and Mexican until my first day of junior high school.

As part of a federal integration program, I—along with some of my classmates from Murchison Elementary School in East Los Angeles—was bused to a white-dominated school in the suburbs: Mt. Gleason Jr. High School in Sunland-Tujunga. Nervous about leaving my barrio for a strange and white place, I braced myself for the unknown. On the first day of school, after an hour bus ride, our bus came "under fire" from rocks hurled by the local white kids. While at some level I was relieved to temporarily escape my impoverished and violent barrio—which included a high level of police abuse—I never expected such a hostile reception from the white natives, like their predecessors from Montgomery, Alabama, during the Civil Rights Movement of the 19050s.

While rocks hurt, so do words. This is especially the case when you're only a twelve-year-old kid. Many years later, I can still recall the racist words hurled by the white teens at us—brown kids from the projects— just like it was yesterday: "Go back to Mexico," "Damn wetbacks," "Dirty Mexicans," "Lazy low-riders," and "F*cking Beaners." To this day, however, I don't understand how calling someone a "low-rider" or "beaner" represented an insult. Doesn't everybody like low-rider cars and beans?

Although I learned from my tough neighborhood and stoic Mexican father to never show fear, it puzzled me that the whites had so much hatred for us? "What did we ever do to them," I asked myself? What does it matter if we have Spanish surnames or if our parents only speak Spanish? Why should they care if we have brown or dark skin? Who cares if I had an accent from East Los Angeles? (Several university degrees later, I probably still have one?) So what if we don't have money or if our parents don't own a home or drive a car?

It didn't take me long to figure out that I was different, where the white teens viewed and treated me as inferior due to the color of my skin, my accent and my zip code (90033, to be exact). For the first time in my life, I realized that I was "a Mexican"—even though I was born in Sacramento, California, and despite spending the first four years of my life in Tijuana (Baja California, Mexico).

For protection or self-defense purposes at "my" white school, I even contemplated joining the neighborhood gang or starting a satellite "gang office" at school. However, given that I was too thin to defend the barrio, I knew that my "gang application" would be rejected. Apparently, I couldn't catch a break as a Chicano teen!

The racism that I, along with my fellow Chicana/o classmates, experienced didn't start or end with the white student. It extended to the school's white-only faculty, administrators and staff. While not as overt as the white students, their racism toward us manifested in forms of paternalism, low expectations and institutional discrimination. For instance, despite graduating at the top of my class and excelling in mathematics at Murchison Elementary School, in junior high school, I was channeled into wood and metal shop classes. At the same time, the white students mostly took music and art classes. With such a low bar for the Chicana/o students to excel, I'm amazed that I didn't join some of my friends in sniffing glue during wood shop—or smoke marijuana during metal shop with some of the misfit white students who "welcomed us"—to escape my bleak reality.

It wasn't just about race; it was also about class. Seeing how the white students arrived to school with their parents in expensive cars—e.g., BMW, Porsche and Mercedes-Benz—I was embarrassed that my Mexican immigrant parents relied on public transportation, since they never owned a car. (It's difficult to own a car when you don't know how to drive or have a driver's license.)

There's no other way of stating my feelings at the time: I was ashamed of being poor and my Mexican immigrant parents. This shame, like a stalker, followed me for many years.

By the time I transferred to Lincoln High School, a Chicana/o-dominated school in Los Angeles, I thought that I had escaped racism. Little did I know that my overcrowded, public high school also had low expectations for the Mexican students. Excelling in the classroom, especially when it came to reading and writing, along with pursuing higher education, were foreign to me and my homeboys from East Los Angeles. The only thing that I knew back then about the university consisted of watching UCLA football games on television.

It wasn't until a childhood friend pressured me to apply (and eventually be accepted) to Upward Bound at Occidental College (Oxy)—a college prep program for historically disadvantaged high school students to pursue higher education—when college became a viable option for the first time in my life.

To make a long story short, if not for key K–12 teachers (like Ms. Cher at Murchison and Mr. Wong at Lincoln), my acceptance to Upward Bound at Oxy, my advanced mathematic skills, the unconditional love from my Mexican parents (Salomon Chavez Huerta and Carmen Mejia Huerta), the support from my siblings and, later, my wise Chicana wife (Antonia Montes), I wouldn't have been able to escape the poverty and violence of my youth to pursue higher education, allowing me to become a published author, public policy expert, public intellectual and professor—where I teach, advise and mentor tomorrow's leaders.

At the end of the day, I only hope that my story of resilience—derived from my working-class background, proud Mexican heritage and the mean streets of East Los Angeles—inspires others with similar experiences to accomplish their dreams.

FIVE

Once Ashamed of My Mexican Parents, but not Anymore

Dr. Alvaro Huerta

When I first applied to UCLA, I wrote in my personal essay that I didn't have any positive role models in my violent neighborhood. Having grown up in East Los Angeles, I wrote that that the majority of the adults consisted of gang members, drug dealers, prostitutes, thieves, *tecatos* (heroin addicts), alcoholics, felons and high school dropouts (or push-outs). I also wrote about my disdain for housing authority officials and government workers for behaving like prison wardens and guards toward us: project residents who depended on subsided public housing and government aid or welfare. Moreover, I decried the police abuse that I witnessed and experienced, like the time when a cop pointed a gun at me. My alleged "crime" consisted of being a fifteen-year-old Chicano making a rolling stop, while learning how to drive.

Moreover, as a product of mostly poor and overcrowded public schools, I highlighted the low expectations that the mostly white teachers and counselors, with some exceptions, for the Chicana/o kids from the public housing projects. Fortunately for me, I excelled in mathematics. Apparently, unlike my childhood friends who eventually joined the local gang (Big Hazard), ended up dead, went jail or became low-wage workers, I ended up being one of the "good Mexican kids." This is a label that I reject! I was neither better nor more "special" than my childhood home-boys.

While I was eventually accepted to UCLA, as a freshman (majoring in mathematics), I should've been more truthful in my essay. In fact, I did have positive role models: my Mexican immigrant parents. But why didn't I give them credit? Did they represent the so-called burdens of society that many American leaders and white citizens want us to believe? No.

Did they migrate to this country to take jobs from American workers? No. My father, Salomon Chavez Huerta, first arrived in this country as a farmworker during the Bracero Program—the U.S.-Mexico guest worker program of the mid-twentieth century. He later worked as a janitor and day laborer.

My mother, Carmen Mejia Huerta, worked as a domestic worker for more than forty years, cleaning the homes and taking care of the children of privileged American families. Like millions of Mexican immigrants, my late parents took jobs that most American workers reject(ed) due to dismal pay, lack of upward mobility and low social status or stigma (i.e., immigrant jobs).

In retrospect, I should've written about their remarkable stories of hard work, sacrifice and resilience in a racist and hostile society. It's amazing how two Spanish-speaking parents, with no formal education, from a small Mexican *rancho* raised eight children, sending four of them to the university. This includes raising the most accomplished artist of Mexican/Latin American origin in the history of the United States: Salomon Huerta. (I'm primarily referring to U.S.-raised Latina/o artists.) After receiving his B.F.A. from Art Center College of Design in Pasadena and M.F.A. from UCLA, my older brother exhibited in the most prestigious galleries and museums in the world. And let's not forget about my younger brothers, Noel and Ismael, who attended UCSB. (Unfortunately, while living in Mexico, my older sisters—Catalina, Soledad and Ofelia—were forced to drop out of school at young age in order to work to help support the family. They also helped raise their younger siblings, including myself, while their/my parents also worked.)

Instead of being proud of my Mexican parents, I was ashamed of their low social status. Actually, since I grew up in a segregated Chicana/o neighborhood where all of the residents received government aid, like many of my childhood friends, I never thought about issues related to race or class. As a kid, I assumed that all parents spoke Spanish and all kids wore hand-me-down clothes and shoes. I also considered food stamps to be the common currency for all Americans to purchase groceries.

It wasn't until being bused to a white junior high school, Mt. Gleason Jr. High, in the suburbs of Los Angeles (Sunland-Tujunga) when I first experienced overt racism and realized that I was poor and Mexican. For the first time, I was different than most people. Not only was I different, but I was also labeled as inferior by my white classmates.

This idea of being different or inferior followed me to the university. I will never forget my first summer class, for instance, when the professor asked the students to share about our parents. While we had other racialized minorities in the class, I was the only Chicana/o student from the mean streets of East Los Angeles.

"Both of my parents are Harvard alums and they're attorneys," an African American student said with pride.

"My mom is a doctor and father is an engineer," a Latina student boasted.

"I'm a foreign exchange student from Latin America, where my father is a diplomat," another student said with delight.

The more my classmates spoke about their parents' stellar resumes, I started to panic. "What should I say," I thought to myself? "Should I say that my mother cleans homes for a living?" "Should I admit that my father sweeps floors in a factory?" "Should I confess that we're on welfare since their meager wages can't feed their eight kids?" All of these questions raced through my confused mind.

Not being able to compete with my privileged classmates and their highly successful parents, I uttered something stupid and general, like "My parents are workers in the U.S."

In short, I was embarrassed of my parents!

To the present, I will never forgive myself for not giving my Mexican parents credit for motivating me to pursue higher education. However, growing up in a society where brown people have become convenient scapegoats for America's woes, it makes sense that I would feel embarrassed about my Mexican roots and working-class background.

While Mexicans in *el norte* have become easy targets for American politicians, there's a long tradition of Mexican-bashing or anti-Mexicanism in the United States. Since the military defeat of Mexico in 1848 (and, before that, the *gringo* invasion of Texas in the early 1800s), American leaders and white citizens have treated Mexicans in this country as second-class citizens, social burdens and national security threats.

As the largest racialized group in this country, accounting for more than 57.5 million citizens/residents, and contributing greatly to this country's advancement, Latinas/os deserve to be treated with dignity and respect.

As a Chicano scholar, who, as a teen, internalized the pejorative narratives against brown people and the working-class in this country, I have a clear message to all Chicanas/os and Latinas/os, especially the youth: Don't allow bullies, like many American leaders and citizens, to make you feel inferior due to your ethnic heritage and social status.

SIX

A Chicana/o Manifesto on Community Organizing

Reflections of a Scholar-Activist

Dr. Alvaro Huerta

As an urban planning and ethnic studies scholar with an extensive background in community and student activism—over the past three decades—I've become an expert in the field of community organizing. While some individuals are experts in the theory of community organizing, they lack the practice. Similarly, while other individuals are experts in the practice of community organizing, they lack the theory. In what I call the "dialectic of community organizing," I possess both the theory and practice. Throughout my life-long efforts to transform the world for the better, I've coined this concept based on the teachings and writings of the late educator and philosopher, Paulo Freire. In his classic book, *Pedagogy of the Oppressed*, the brilliant Freire argues for a liberating education: "Liberation is a praxis: the action and reflection of men and women upon the world in order to transform it" (79).

Since 1985, starting as a freshman at UCLA, I've studied social movements and revolutions—domestically and internationally. This included studying the theoretical foundations and leaders behind major societal transformations throughout the world, such as the revolutions in America, Mexico, Russia, China and Cuba. Supplementing my university studies, during the mid-1980s, I engaged in student activism as a proud member of MEChA (*Movimiento Estudiantil Chicano de Aztlán*). This included advocating for U.S. divestment in South Africa's apartheid regime, promoting racial and economic diversity in higher education and defending the rights of undocumented students. While not one of the five hunger strikers, I played a leadership role in a student hunger strike at UCLA (November 11–19, 1987) for undocumented students. During this historic hunger strike, we successfully fought to continue university funding and other services for undocumented students on campus. Our victorious efforts provided an organizing model for other Chicana/o student activists to stage similar hunger strikes at UCLA (May 24 to June 7, 1993) and UCSB (April 27 to May 5, 1994), among other campuses.

At the community level, I—along with fellow activists (Adrian Alvarez, Antonia Montes, Karina Prado, Elsa Bolado, Leticia Sanchez, Pedro Perez, etc.) and Latino immigrant gardeners (Jaime Aleman, Roberto Cabrera, Antonio Alamillo, Jose M. Perez, etc.)—co-founded the Association of Latin American Gardeners of Los Angeles (ALAGLA). We founded ALAGLA to challenge the City of Los Angeles' leaf blower ban—signed into law by a 9–3 margin on December 3, 1996. This draconian ban included a misdemeanor charge, $1,000 fine and up to six months in jail for Latino gardeners cited for using a leaf blower within 500 feet of a residential area. (Conveniently for the city, the ban excluded city gardeners in non-residential areas.) Learning from the UCLA's hunger strike of 1987, during the pivotal period of ALAGLA's grassroots campaign, eleven organizers/members staged a six-day hunger strike in front of City Hall (January 3–9, 1998) to demand justice for honest, hardworking Latino gardeners (Huerta and Morales 80).

Following this dynamic grassroots campaign, as the lead organizer at Communities for Better Environment (CBE)—during the late 1990s and early 2000s—I successfully led an organizing campaign to defeat a proposed power plant in Southeast Los Angeles—specifically, the City of South Gate. If built, the proposed power plant—the size of Dodger Stadium—would have emitted over 150 tons of pollution per year, such as particulate matter (PM10) (Huerta 96). PM10 (or fine particles of soot) has been linked to premature death, including heart failure and respiratory ailments, such as asthma and bronchitis.

For the record, all successful community-based campaigns represent collective efforts, where all participants (e.g., leadership, membership, volunteers, sympathizers) deserve credit.

That said, given my positionality as a scholar-activist and public policy advocate on behalf of *los de abajo*/those on the bottom, I offer my *dos centavos* (or two cents) in a non-ranked order for current and future community organizers to benefit from.

It's imperative for community organizers to learn from current and historical organizing campaigns based on social, racial and economic justice. Since the turbulent 1960s to the present, college/university students have played a key role in protesting unjust wars (e.g., Vietnam, Iraq), eradicating racism, defending free speech, demanding diversity in higher education and fighting for a more just society, among other noble causes. Given their privileged status, college/university students have the luxury of time and access to resources to study contemporary and historical social movements and revolutions. This allows this class or group to learn from influential thinkers and leaders—past and present—responsible for creating transformative change in this country and beyond. While not limited to college/university students, the idea here is for community organizers to also study influential causes and their leaders to be better prepared—theoretically and strategically—for emerging causes or struggles.

It's imperative to demonstrate humility and for organizers to not impose their moral values, when working with or organizing marginalized communities. When organizing marginalized community members or vulnerable groups, like Kendrick Lamar—greatest rapper alive—says, "be humble." Need I say more on this point?

In terms of moral values, it's imperative that community organizers don't impose their own values or belief systems on the community members they're "trying to help." Organizers should not judge or try to change the behavior or actions of community members or presuppose that they know "what's good for the community." (There are exceptions, however, like in the case of heroin addicts, etc.) Be open, listen and engage in dialogue with community members or group members to better understand why individuals or (sub)groups adopt particular behavior, conduct, speech, attire, etc.

Overall, instead of operating from a hierarchal or top-down approach (like some abusive non-profits and unions that I've worked for in past years, such as SEIU-USWW in Los Angeles), engage with community members on a horizontal or an equal level. In other words, don't organize "for" community members; organize "with" them.

While organizing marginalized communities, don't romanticize poverty. There's nothing good about being poor or the objective conditions of the working poor or working-class in this country. I should know since I grew up in abject poverty—both in Tijuana (Baja California, Mexico) and East Los Angeles (California, U.S.), as I articulated in my TEDx talk on April 27, 2017. Thus, community organizers shouldn't shy away from improving the living conditions or neighborhoods of historically disenfranchised groups.

What's important, however, is to improve or invest in these communities without the perils of gentrification or displacement of the same people you're "trying to help." For instance, the urban renewal program of twentieth century—supposedly aimed at "improving" and "transforming cities"—caused havoc for racialized groups and working-class communities in America's barrios and ghettos.

Access the existing social networks of marginalized communities and build from these networks. While racialized and working-class communities may be "poor" in terms of financial capital, they are often "rich" in terms of social networks and other forms of social capital. Social networks constitute interpersonal connections among family members, friends, acquaintances, neighbors, co-workers and other relationships, like those via the church (e.g., *padrinos/madrinas, compadres/comadres*). In the case of many Chicana/o-Latina/o households, we can clearly see how they effectively organize themselves (and maintain their cultures/identities) around important family events and celebrations, like weddings, *quinceañeras*, baptisms, *Dia de los Muertos* and so on.

Moreover, to effectively organize and mobilize these communities or members around particular campaigns or key issues (e.g., legalize street vending, halt deportations, defeat gentrification, challenge draconian laws), it's important for community organizers to access their pre-existing networks. For instance, when a small group of Chicana/o activists, as mentioned above, organized Latino immigrant gardeners—an informal labor niche that had never successfully been organized before—to defeat a draconian leaf blower ban, the activists did so by accessing and building on the social networks (or migrant networks) of Jaime Aleman—a veteran gardener from Zacatecas, Mexico.

I will never forget that cold Saturday night in the summer of 1996, when we—Adrian, Pedro and myself—first met with some of Jaime's *paisanos* and fellow gardeners behind an overcrowded apartment building. By tapping into Jaime's networks and initiating/creating bonds between the activists and gardeners, we launched a successful campaign against City Hall. By chance, like qualitative researchers, we used this opportunity or insider access to initiate snowball sampling strategies to obtain referrals or contacts with other gardeners throughout the greater Los Angeles area.

It's key to build confianza or trust among marginalized communities. Without establishing or building *confianza* (or trust) between community organizers and community members or impacted groups, the organizers will fail miserably. *Confianza* isn't something you can establish overnight. It takes time to establish and build. It also takes patience, honesty, transparency, consistency and good deeds on behalf of the organizers. Too often, marginalized community members have been taken advantage of by opportunists, politicians, hustlers, hucksters, researchers, etc., in this country and, for some, in their home countries. This is one reason why marginalized community members are suspicious of outsiders, despite the good intentions of organizers to help improve their plight.

Thus, before any community organizer arrives into a community or neighborhood that they're not embedded in and begin to demand or request action or participation by the community members, the organizers must first get to know the people, especially on a social or personal level. This includes attending events or places where community members congregate, like schools, churches and parks. It helps to start with one person or family and build *confianza* from there. It's impossible to deliver a political speech at a local school or church, expecting community members to trust you or your good intentions. On a similar note, it's a waste of time, money and energy to distribute flyers, expecting for community members to join your cause without making or creating relationships with them.

Don't forget to eat the tacos de carnitas. Should a community organizer be fortunate enough to be invited into the home of a Latina/o community member or to attend a special occasion, like a *quinceañera*, don't offend the host(s) by rejecting their food. In many Mexican households—both in this country and their communities of origin—the host(s) will often serve their guests food and drink without asking. This applies to the poorest barrios of California, U.S., to the poorest villages of Chiapas, Mexico. Thus, should the guest(s) refuse to eat the served food or drink, the host(s) will often be offended. This is no way of building *confianza*!

When organizing against the power plant proposal in South Gate, I noticed some of my fellow organizers, particularly the youth, commit this "crime" or insult due to their vegetarian or vegan diets. I tried to compensate by ordering some extra *tacos de carnitas* to go, but the damage had already been done.

Organizing at cantinas and Mexican restaurants. Community organizing shouldn't be limited to distributing flyers, holding press conferences and organizing protests. Community organizing should also include socializing at bars, restaurants, coffee shops and back-yard *carne asada* cookouts with community members. When organizing gardeners, as Chicana/o activists, we established strong personal relationships with the Latino immigrant gardeners—mostly from rural Mexico—over some beers, particularly Pacifico and Dos Equis. (Actually, "some" is an understatement.) This is an insightful point that Adrian Alvarez, as president of ALAGLA, articulated at a symposium held on May 13, 2018 at UCLA's Chicano Studies Research Center (CSRC): "Organizing Latino Immigrants in the Informal Economy: The Successful Case of the Association of Latin American Gardeners of Los Angeles."

Organizers should immerse yourself fully into their campaign. When organizing a grassroots campaign, the organizer must immerse herself or himself fully, maintaining focus on the particular campaign without distractions. Too often, organizers spread themselves too thin by taking on too many campaigns or issues at the same time. This is a recipe for failure. When I co-organized the gardeners or led the campaign against the power plant, I immersed myself fully without internal or external distractions. This allowed me to focus on my particular leadership role within the given organizing campaign and its objectives.

While there are psychological and physical costs to being immersed or committed fully to a challenging organizing campaign or cause, where the organizer is constantly thinking about the opponents (e.g., corporation, City Hall, federal government) and major obstacles, etc., this is the price the committed organizer pays for fighting the good fight and dreaming for a better world!

I end with the profound words of Ricardo Flores Magón (1920)—the precursor of the Mexican Revolution: *". . . prefiero ser un soñador que un hombre práctico"* (141).

SEVEN

"Just Say No" to the Senate's "Gang of Eight" Immigration Bill

Dr. Alvaro Huerta

On April 17, 2013, as part of the Senate's so-called "Gang of Eight," Senator Chuck Schumer, D-NY, introduced S. 77 or the "Border Security, Economic Opportunity, and Immigration Modernization Act." This 844-page document represented a complex, costly, enforcement-centered and morally bankrupt bill. (The other Senators of this gang included: Michael Bennet, D-CO; Dick Durbin, D-IL; Jeff Flake, R-AZ; John McCain, R-AZ; Robert Mendez, D-NJ; and Marco Rubio, R-FL). Given the national debate over this so-called immigration reform bill, I have one recommendation for this bi-partisan group of Senators: go back to the drawing board.

To start, let's take the case of the "path to citizenship" component. It makes no sense why undocumented immigrants should pay exorbitant costs, such as financial penalties, back taxes and application fees? Haven't these immigrants suffered enough financial hardships with the epidemic wage-theft that they experience in the workplace? What about the case that immigrant workers, too often, toil below the minimum wage, receiving no over-time, adequate lunch breaks and other basic work-place rights that most citizens enjoy? Also, don't employers and consumers already benefit from these mostly low-wage workers, while purchasing basic goods and services on a daily basis? What about all the taxes that immigrants pay—directly and indirectly—without benefiting from federal programs, such as government assistance, Social Security and Medicare?

Moreover, the border-enforcement pre-requisite before anyone qualifies for citizenship illustrates the absurd aspect of this bill. Why do undocumented immigrants have to pay for something, such as border control, that's out of their control? How will immigration officials accurately know that the established 90 percent apprehension success goal will ever be met? As a social scientist, for example, I can't know 90 percent of anything unless I know the universe of the population that I'm studying.

This pre-requisite is designed for failure because there's no guarantee that immigration officials or the proposed bi-partisan task force will ever agree that the border is 90 percent secure due to economic and/or political reasons. It's also immoral because it only creates the illusion or false hope for millions of honest, hard-working immigrants—who contribute more than their fair share to this country—of one day becoming American citizens.

The proposed thirteen-year wait period for undocumented immigrants to be eligible for citizenship only occurs (if at all) after a five-year period, when immigration officials will determine if the U.S.-Mexico border is found to be 90 percent secure. If not, the proposed bi-partisan task force will take control, study the issue and make recommendations. This idiotic and inhumane bureaucratic process only creates unpredictable outcomes for the aspiring citizens.

In short, to borrow from the late First Lady Nancy Reagan's catchy phrase of the war on drugs policy during the 1980s, President Barack Obama, Congress and the public should "Just Say No" to the Gang of Eight's draconian immigration bill. In lieu of this cruel bill, we need a new immigration bill guided by humanistic principles with one central component: amnesty.

EIGHT

No White Christmas
for Brown Immigrants

Dr. Alvaro Huerta

On December 11, 2013, the political controversy created by Megyn Kelly—the media darling of Fox News—where she told American kids on the air that Santa "is just white," rings truthful for millions of brown immigrants in this country. Latina/o immigrants, specifically those who lack legal status, will have something less to celebrate in 2013, once again, since neither President Barack Obama nor Congress took meaningful action to resolve their precarious and vulnerable status.

In a season of holiday celebrations, when millions of families gather to feast on food, open presents and "count their blessings," Obama continues to deport undocumented immigrants at record rates, whereby separating families apart. According to data from Immigration and Customs Enforcement (ICE), the Obama administration had deported over two million immigrants in the past five years. Compared to former U.S. Presidents, this mark makes Obama the leader in the field of separating families and penalizing mostly honest, hard-working individuals for the simple act of wanting a better future for themselves and their families.

While Obama supported a 2013 bi-partisan, immigration bill drafted by the so-called "Senate Gang of Eight," where it passed in the Senate and stalled in the House, the House-dominated Republicans balked on a so-called pathway to citizenship plan for undocumented immigrants. Although Democratic leaders in Congress and some immigrant advocacy groups begrudge Republicans for not acting on this so-called "comprehensive immigration reform" bill, this draconian legislation is politically and ethically flawed for undocumented immigrants and their families. By focusing mainly on enforcement and security measures, such as the militarization of the U.S.-Mexico border with thousands of additional enforcement agents, high-tech reinforcement and expansion of the wall, increased drones and military-related equipment, not to mention cruel employer-based measures to identify and deport undocumented workers, this bill does more harm than good for those who live and work in America's shadows.

If Obama and Congress truly want to make progress in fixing the dysfunctional immigration system and not just penalize those on the bottom, Democratic and Republican leaders should accept the premise that undocumented immigrants represent mostly honest, hard-working individuals who contribute greatly to this country's prosperity. While it's politically convenient to blame Latina/o immigrants for America's economic ills, why don't America's leaders and the public, especially white folks, recognize their strong work ethic and daily sacrifice when they clean houses, raise children, care for the elderly, mow lawns, wash dishes, park cars, sell delicious food on the streets and sell their labor on street corners?

When Obama speaks about "American exceptionalism" in international affairs, he should seriously re-examine his domestic policies and how his administration treats the most vulnerable and exploited among us. Is there anything "exceptional" about deporting human beings and ripping families apart? As the leader of the most powerful nation in the world, Obama has enormous executive powers that he needs to exercise to help vulnerable groups by providing permanent relief for undocumented immigrants living and working in this country. It's not enough to provide temporary relief to some undocumented youth or so-called DREAMers, Obama also should immediately halt the deportations and detention of all undocumented immigrants (except for serious criminals, like murderers and water-boarders) until Congress passes true comprehensive immigration reform based on humane principles, like dignity and respect for all. If Obama is truly concerned with criminals, what about deporting war criminals, such as former Secretary of State Henry Kissinger?

Obama should also act to prevent the senseless deaths of Latina/o immigrants who attempt to cross border states, resulting in an "invisible" humanitarian crisis in this country. During the past decade, over 2,000 immigrants have died in border states. In Arizona's deserts, for example, many immigrants, lacking water and shade, succumb to dehydration and extreme heat exposure. The estimated deaths only includes those bodies that have been found, where families from Mexico and Central America mourn their dead and missing relatives. Where's the public outcry in America for brown people? Who will fight and defend the interests of these human beings and future ones in their treacherous journey, if not the government with its financial, technological and humanitarian resources at its disposal?

For those immigrants who survive the brutal U.S.-Mexico border crossing, many of them face a nightmarish experience after being apprehended and imprisoned by ICE agents. Operated by public officials and for-profit interests, detention centers or immigrant prisons serve the function to criminalize, punish, detain and deport immigrants with minimal rights and limited access to legal counsel. Too often, unaware or misinformed of their rights, many immigrants sign stipulated orders of removal, waiving their right to a hearing in front of a judge to plead their case. Moreover, given that these men and women are desperate to escape their harsh imprisonment, by signing this "voluntary" deportation form, many of them are unaware of the legal ramifications, such as "agreeing" to a ten-year restriction on re-entry to the U.S. and other punitive consequences.

Once again, I find nothing "exceptional" about how the U.S. government treats those who work and live in America's shadows. Thus, by taking decisive and just actions toward resolving the dysfunctional immigration system and treating immigrants humanely, Obama should remind Kelly and her friends at Fox News that Santa doesn't have to be white, after all.

NINE

Lessons on Community Organizing in Chicana/o Communities

Educate, Agitate, and Organize

Dr. Alvaro Huerta

As a former resident of Boyle Heights, I first started organizing on behalf of Chicanas/os (and Latinas/os) in 1985, as a student activist at UCLA. By attending an elite university, I quickly realized that not many students on campus came from working-class neighborhoods and, especially, public housing projects, like I did. More specifically, I was surprised that most of my Latina/o classmates never experienced similar hardships that I did growing up in a segregated barrio plagued by abject poverty, police abuse, high unemployment rates, disproportionate incarceration rates, drug addiction and violence. While on campus, I also started to reflect on my old neighborhood and its built environment—surrounded by freeways, railroad tracks and shuttered factories. Based on these objective conditions and the Chicana/o history that I learned in the classroom, I became an agent for transformative change on behalf of marginalized communities—my people.

Thus, after leaving the university, I became a community organizer. As a community organizer, I played a leading role in grassroots campaigns against bad policies impacting Chicanas/os in general and Mexican immigrants, such as a draconian law against Latino gardeners (i.e., Los Angeles's draconian lead blower ban) and proposal for a polluting power plant in South Gate—a predominately working-class, Latina/o city.

Currently, as a scholar-activist, I'm in a more privileged position to reflect, research and provide insight on key lessons that I've learned over the years on effective community organizing in Latina/o communities. While electoral changes are necessary to ensure basic rights (e.g., affordable housing, universal healthcare), grassroots organizing in working class-communities serves to create transformative social change, as these constituencies have concrete solutions, from the ground up, for the socio-economic issues impacting them based on their lived experiences.

Originally coined by the late Indian jurist and politician, B.R. Ambedkar, of the early to mid-1900s, social movement building can be categorized or spearheaded by three key typologies: (1) Educate; (2) Agitate; and (3) Organize.

Educate. Before we—those of us interested in justice and equality for all—engage in community organizing or want to launch a grassroots campaign against any form of injustice by powerful interests or leaders, we must first educate ourselves about the particular problem and its history. This is an ongoing process, however, where we must continually educate ourselves on the particular issue that we're dealing with. If we're concerned with gentrification/displacement of working class communities of color in Los Angeles, such as in the city's districts of Highland Park, Echo Park and Boyle Heights, we must first educate ourselves about the local history of demographic and economic changes over time, especially pertaining to the plight of Chicanas/os, African Americans and other racialized groups.

Moreover, by studying U.S. history in general and Los Angeles history in particular since the early twentieth century, we learn that government officials and private interests (e.g., developers, bankers, real estate agents) worked in conjunction to marginalize racialized communities. This was done by racist government policies and practices, such as redlining, where so-called blighted, undesirable and high-risk neighborhoods were designated for people of color. Additionally, we learn that during the post–WWII era, government-led urban renewal programs and private interests, resulted in the concentration of racialized communities in the inner-cities, such as barrios and ghettos.

Simultaneously, while Latinas/os, African Americans and other racialized groups were relegated to the inner-cities, these same racist forces facilitated for whites to flee to the suburbs (i.e., white flight.). Federally funded freeways, connecting whites from the inner-cities to the suburbs also facilitated white flight. And let's not forget the low-interest loans for whites to move into suburban housing developments and the racist attitudes white residents held against people of color, denying them the opportunities to diversity American suburbia.

During the past couple of decades, however, we're witnessing "reverse white flight," where whites are leaving the suburbs and returning to the cities. This includes the inner-cities, where they're displacing the same communities of color that previous generations of whites left behind to live in despair/misery. This is a national trend, where we see major cities, like San Francisco and New York, also experiencing gentrification.

Agitate. As we can clearly see from the African American civil rights movement, transformative social change occurs when the afflicted (and allies) rise up to agitate against those in power. From Rosa Parks refusing to give up her seat in Montgomery, Alabama, to the Greensboro Four who endured abuse to desegregate lunch counters in Greensboro, North Carolina, to countless sacrifices led by liberation groups (e.g., Black Panther Party), we clearly see that transformative change only occurs when the victimized/oppressed protest, march, boycott, write and organize to demand their human and civil rights in this country.

While not as well documented as the historic actions led by African Americans, Chicanas/os—led primarily by the youth, such as the Brown Berets—in East Los Angeles and beyond also organized against the capitalist system with non-violent acts or actions to demand for transformative social change. During the late 1960s, Chicana/o students from several high schools—including Lincoln, Wilson, Roosevelt, Garfield and Belmont—walked out of their classes to protest the Los Angeles School District's (LAUSD's) racist policies in public schools. This includes the absence of Mexican American studies, lack of bilingual education, punishment for speaking Spanish, lack of college-bound classes, hostile/abusive campus conditions (e.g., no access to restrooms during lunch) and school-related issues. While the walk outs represented non-violent acts, the police forces and legal system used excessive force and imprisonment against the protesting student leaders, including the late Chicano teacher and charismatic leader Sal Castro.

Yet, we don't need to go back to the 1960s to learn about current social movements taking place by brown and black community activists, fighting for immigration rights, affordable housing, responsible development and higher paying jobs. This also includes challenging gentrification and ending police abuse in communities of color in Los Angeles and throughout the country.

Organize. When powerful interests or leaders impose harsh laws against racialized groups, members of these impacted communities have no choice but to organize for self-determination. This organizing imperative must be led by the same members of the impacted communities, following the fine examples of the Brown Berets and Black Panthers.

Marginalized communities can't wait for the "great white hope" or "great white savior," such as the next John F. Kennedy (JFK), to rescue them from their objective conditions. Actually, it not need be a white leader, as millions of historically marginalized voters learned the hard way when electing President Barack Obama, as the first African American leader of the most powerful nation in the world, foolishly thinking that all of their/our socio-economic problems, etc., would be solved. While elections do matter, communities of color in particular must always look from within their communities—keeping their organic leaders accountable—to defend their interests. In order to free themselves from their oppressive conditions, they must organize themselves and collaborate with seasoned organizers/activists. This must be done or achieved under the premise of self-determination in order for those on the margins to make transformative changes in their communities and society via educating, agitating and organizing.

TEN

Socioeconomic Inequality Impacting Marginalized Communities Must Change

Dr. Alvaro Huerta

It's official: the topic of income equality is in vogue. From researchers to cable talk show hosts, from policy makers to civic leaders, it seems like everyone is talking about the economic disparities between affluent and low- to middle-income earners in the United States. In fact, the popular romance book, "Fifty Shades of Grey"—by the British author E. L. James—was defeated by the 2013 book, "Capital in the Twenty-First Century"—by the French economist Thomas Piketty—on many bestseller lists, including Amazon. While those who generate knowledge and draft public policies suddenly became enlightened about income inequality and its negative impacts on economically disadvantaged groups, throughout U.S. history, Latinas/os have experienced the pernicious nature of being at the bottom end of America's socioeconomic ladder.

Latinas/os, as the nation's largest racialized group, work in all sectors of the economy. While employed in an array of sectors, according to statistics from a 2011 American Community Survey, on average, the Latina/o household income at $39,000 was lower than the national average at $50,000. Also, on average, the Latina/o poverty rate at 26 percent was higher than the national average at 16 percent. These unequal figures reflect the types of jobs that Latinas/os hold, where pay is typically lower than the national average. For example, this commonly includes blue-collar, service sector jobs with low pay and limited upward mobility opportunities. This is not to imply, however, that all Latinas/os hold blue-collar jobs. I, for instance, hold university degrees from elite universities and am an academic.

In addition to below-average household income, Latinas/os experienced additional economic hardships as a result of the Great Recession—starting in December of 2007—and its lingering impacts. According to the Pew Research Center, in 2011, while the national homeownership rate among whites was at 73.7 percent, for Asians, it was at 58.1 percent. For Latina/os, the homeownership rate was 47.4 percent, somewhat higher compared with African Americans, at 25.1 percent. Given the importance of homeownership in the United States, as a valuable asset of accumulated wealth for the owners and their offspring, these percentage differences only perpetuate economic and racial inequality in this country.

As major contributors of the housing crisis during the Great Recession, according to Dr. Peter Dreier in a *New York Times'* op-ed titled "What Housing Recovery?," banks and mortgage brokers practiced risky, irresponsible and, often, illegal lending toward home borrowers, leading up to and during the Great Recession. More specifically, banks and mortgage brokers frequently persuaded potential buyers to obtain variable interest loans and, more insidious, high-interest subprime loans with the false premise that the new homeowner could refinance in the near future at a fixed and lower rate, which contributed to a housing bubble. These greedy and unethical schemes had disproportionately negative impacts on Latinas/os and African communities. In 2006, according to Dreier, during the height of subprime lending, whites made up 18 percent of those who received these risky loans, compared to 47 percent of Latinas/os and 54 percent of African Americans.

As a result of these nefarious lending and financial practices, banks and mortgage brokers were mainly responsible for many home foreclosures and underwater mortgages—where homeowners owe more to the bank or lender than the current home value.

As a means of improving upward mobility opportunities among Latinas/os, many academics, policymakers, community activists and civic leaders argue in favor of raising the minimum wage, producing more affordable housing, improving public schools, increasing taxes on the wealthy and implementing comprehensive immigration reform.

Moreover, there seems to be a growing consensus among Latina/o leaders and academics for public and private agencies to invest in disenfranchised Latina/o communities in order for this racialized group to become more competitive in a highly advanced society. This should be done with holistic, innovative and forward-thinking approaches to deep-rooted socioeconomic problems that have plagued Latinas/os for many generations, such as residing in impoverished and segregated neighborhoods, attending sub-par public schools, being confined to low-wage occupations and lacking equal access to higher education.

As the fastest-growing segment of the American workforce as of 2014, with an estimated 25 million workers or 16 percent of wage earners—not to mention their countless historical contributions to this country—Latinas/os deserve all of the benefits and rights this country has to offer. This includes, but not limited to, the right for all Latinas/os to access affordable housing, safe neighborhoods, well-paying jobs and excellent educational opportunities. Anything less from these basic needs and rights to survive and thrive in this country only perpetuates the status quo, where Latinas/os remain at the bottom of the income and racial inequality equation.

FIVE WAYS TO BRIDGE INCOME INEQUALITY

During the early 2010s, the national political discourse about income inequality prevailed among American leaders, policy makers and the mainstream media. How long will it take before American leaders do something about it? As the rich have gotten richer, the rest of us have fallen behind—especially Latinas/os. "From 2005 to 2009, the median level of home equity held by Hispanic homeowners declined by half—from $99,983 to $49,145—while the homeownership rate among Hispanics was also falling, from 51% to 47%," according to a report by the Pew Research Center (March 26, 2011). And during a similar period, the poverty rate for Latinas/os reached 26.6 percent, according to another report by same center (March 28, 2011).

Yet, you don't need to be a low-wage Latina/o worker or an economist to let American leaders know how earning the minimum wage in this country is not enough to purchase a home or rent an affordable apartment in a safe neighborhood. It's also not enough to own a reliable vehicle, purchase insurance, secure health insurance, attend college (without incurring massive debt) and acquire basic goods/services to thrive in this country.

How many homes must a Latina domestic worker clean in order to purchase a laptop computer for her child? How many front lawns must a Latino gardener mow to send his daughter to college?

This is not to imply that all Latinas/os toil in the informal or unregulated economy, like my late parents. Latinas/os, as a heterogeneous group, represent productive individuals in diverse occupational fields within the informal and formal economy, such as the service sector, banking, construction, education, entertainment, legal, media, medical and real estate, just to make a few.

The point is that no one in the United States who works hard and sacrifices daily should be left by the wayside. Thus, aside from replacing capitalism—an inherently unequal, contradictory and exploitative system—I propose five ways to bridge the inequality gap in this country, not just for Latinas/os, but also for all racialized minorities and the worker-class.

First, raise the minimum wage to a living wage.

Second, produce more affordable housing.

Third, invest more on public K–12 education. This includes creating smaller class sizes, paying teachers' higher salaries, providing teachers with the adequate resources and teaching assistance that they need to succeed

Fourth, make public colleges/universities tuition-free for all.

Fifth, increase taxes on the income and accumulated wealth of the rich.

In short, all residents, regardless of the color of their skin or legal status, deserve their fair share of the elusive American Dream.

ELEVEN

Republican Leaders Will Regret Attacking Latina/o Immigrants

Dr. Alvaro Huerta

The Republican Party hurt itself by taking comprehensive immigration reform off the table in early 2014. During this period, the Republican leadership announced that it was killing any possibility of comprehensive immigration reform during this year's mid-term election year. This political calculation was counter to the party's desire to court the Latina/o vote—a growing political force to be reckoned with. And it marked a hasty turnaround.

Going against the interests of Latinas/os, Republican leaders in Congress introduced a package of principles centered on draconian immigration reform. This package included recycled conservative policies of punitive enforcement measures, such as enhanced border security, advanced tracking system, employer-based verification, legal reforms, some "relief" for "qualified" undocumented youth and a vague form of legal status for those who qualify.

These harsh and deeply flawed principles excluded a key component for the estimated 11 million undocumented immigrants: a pathway to citizenship. By abandoning a pathway to citizenship plan, the Republican leadership settled to do nothing meaningful. As a consequence, it dashed whatever remaining fantasies Republicans had of gaining political or electoral ground with Latinas/os. Ironically, Republicans had an opening to attack President Barack Obama on this issue. While Obama deported more than two million undocumented immigrants, he continued to militarize the U.S.–Mexico border—two unpopular policies with Latinas/os. Yet, by shirking comprehensive immigration reform, a key issue for Latinas/os, the Republican leadership let Obama and the Democratic Party off the hook.

The Republican leadership, which included House Speaker John Boehner (R-OH), House Majority Leader Eric Cantor (R-VA) and Rep. Paul Ryan (R-WI), capitulated to the extremists in their party and to cowardly House Republicans who dreaded to be challenged from anti-immigrant tea party candidates. This is not to imply that Boehner and company are neither extremists nor cowards. Essentially, these so-called leaders gave their colleagues who were vulnerable some cover by choosing not to put the issue on the agenda. Thus, the stranglehold that the extreme right had—and has—on the GOP prevented it from moving forward with meaningful immigration reform. The party selected, once again, petty politics over the public good.

By not addressing the needs of Latinas/os, the GOP leadership continued to disrespect this important and diverse racialized group. It was also acting in a self-destructive way by disregarding the demographic changes occurring in this country. Or, as I, along with others argue, it looks like some powerful white people fear the browning of America. With an estimated population of 57.5 million, Latinas/os constitute the largest racialized minority in America, with a growing presence all across the country.

Then-President George W. Bush and his extremist adviser Karl Rove understood the need to reach out to Latina/o voters for political reasons. This was something that was lost on former Governor Mitt Romney in the 2012 presidential election. Romney's anti-immigrant views—remember "self-deporting"?—helped propel three-fourths of Latinas/os to vote for Obama.

It looks like the Republicans still haven't learned this lesson. They stand to lose more Latina/o voters. And if they continue to disrespect Latinas/os, they will pay the price, again, in future elections. Fortunately for America, by following this path, the GOP (or Grand Old Party) will eventually become the Grand Obsolete Party.

GOP'S LEGAL TACTICS AGAINST LATINA/O IMMIGRANTS HURT THE PARTY

In early 2015, Republican leaders reached a new low point by using the judiciary to attack Latina/o immigrants. As part of their failed offensive against then-President Barack Obama's immigration executive order aimed at parents, Deferred Action for Parental Accountability (DAPA), which would've provided temporary deportation relief for an estimated 5 million immigrants, Republicans resorted to the courts to block this desperately needed program. Consequently, Republican governors from twenty-six states won a temporary federal injunction in South Texas from

U.S. District Judge Andrew Hanen. It's no coincidence that these governors found a friend in the conservative Judge Hanen, who was appointed to the court by then-President George W. Bush.

The Obama administration thereafter sought to overturn this temporary injunction through the appeals court. But with their judicial recourse, Republican leaders have sent a clear message to all Latinas/os: there's no room for brown people in the GOP. And this clear and loud message is not only being heard by Latinas/os, but also by other racialized groups with large immigrant populations, such as Asian and Pacific Islanders. Asian and Pacific Islanders consist of 1.5 million of the over 11 million undocumented immigrants in this country.

Simultaneously, the GOP also aimed at eliminating Obama's first immigration executive order to provide temporary deportation for youth under the Deferred Action for Childhood Arrivals (DACA) program. They also aimed at increasing the deportations of undocumented immigrants, which was already extremely high under the Obama administration.

Since Obama, like his predecessors, had legal authority to implement executive orders without congressional approval, then-House Speaker John Boehner (R-OH) and fellow Republicans orchestrated to a defunding bill against these immigrant-based programs. In doing so, Boehner behaved like the neighborhood kid with a football who takes the ball home because he doesn't like the rules of the game. Yet, while Republicans had taken control of the Senate during the 2014 elections, they lacked the necessary sixty votes to override Obama's veto power. Thus, on February 5, 2015, the defunding bill died in the Senate, representing the third consecutive defeat.

Obama's move to act on his own outwitted the Republicans by forcing them to take the blame, once again, for the lack of comprehensive immigration reform. After experiencing tremendous heat from undocumented immigrants and their advocates for deporting more than 2 million immigrants, Obama had little choice but to regain the trust of Latinas/os. In response, Republican leaders quickly went on the offensive with their anti-immigrant or xenophobic actions.

Republicans, however, can't maintain their anti-immigrant policies and actions forever, especially given the dramatic demographic changes occurring in the United States. For example, while Latinas/os represent the largest racialized group in the country, Asian and Pacific Islanders consist of the fastest-growing racialized group(s). According to Census data estimates from 2014, while Latinas/os represented over 55 million citizens/residents in this country, Asian and Pacific Islanders consisted of an estimated 20 million citizens/residents. Thus, Republicans can't afford to alienate these important groups and voting blocs, if they ever want to secure the majority of their votes.

California's GOP learned its lesson the hard way when then-Gov. Pete Wilson supported Proposition 187—a 1994 ballot initiative aimed to deny undocumented immigrants essential services. The political fallout has been devastating for Republicans. As a result, they have suffered at the ballot box where Democrats have dominated the governorship, both legislative chambers and vast majority of statewide and federal elected offices. On January 8, 2015, for instance, when then-U.S. Senator Barbara Boxer (D-CA) announced that she would not seek re-election for Congress in 2016, no viable Republican candidates could be found to secure this important. This cautionary tale is one that national GOP leaders should learn from.

If Republicans think that they can survive as a major political party in the future, especially without the majority support of Latinas/os, Asians and Pacific Islanders—not to mention the lack of voter support from African Americans—they will have no one to blame but themselves.

TWELVE

Scaremongering Over Child Refugees is Deplorable

Dr. Alvaro Huerta

In the summer of 2014, we witnessed a national hysteria over unaccompanied child refugees into the United States. I was born in this country, where I was taught that America welcomes immigrants and refugees. But when I saw the ugly protests and heard the racist rants of American citizens, mostly white folks, toward brown immigrants, especially children, I became appalled by the nativist Americans. Growing up in this country, I was always taught that Americans are a generous people, helping the disadvantaged in this country and throughout the world. In elementary school, my teachers taught me basic lessons of common decency. My parents instilled in me with similar values. This includes treating others with respect, telling the truth and having compassion for the less fortunate.

Instead of treating child migrants as human beings or welcoming them as refugees fleeing abject poverty, crime and violence, these Americans recklessly and inhumanely portrayed child migrants as drug smugglers, terrorists, disease-infected individuals and, overall, threats to national security. These are children we're talking about! These acts only blemish America's reputation as a country that prides itself on spreading freedom around the world and providing humanitarian aid, when called upon. They also reveal contempt for the essential American belief that you're innocent until proven guilty. In this country, for instance, you're not supposed label someone a drug smuggler without providing proof.

You're not supposed to link child migrants to so-called terrorist networks without evidence. Someone should've shown former Texas Gov.

Rick Perry, a Republican, a global map to locate the bases of ISIS terrorists, since he claimed, where Perry claims, without any evidence or facts
to prove his case, that these terrorists could be crossing the U.S.-Mexico
border. Let's be clear about something: as a Catholic dominated country
with an efficient police state apparatus, the Mexican government would
never allow for Islamic terrorists to establish bases or networks on Mexican soil!

You're not supposed to assert that child migrants carry diseases without providing hard data of medical examinations and results. Some
elected officials, like then-Rep. Phil Gingrey (R-GA), irresponsibly linked
child migrants to the Ebola virus. In fact, there are no reported cases of
Ebola in Mexico or Central America. At the time, it was plaguing individuals in West Africa.

Instead of helping vulnerable individuals when they're down on their
luck or in desperate need of relief, these Republican leaders behaved like
schoolyard bullies. They picked on weaker and vulnerable individuals
who couldn't defend themselves. This type of cruel and unusual behavior
shows the true colors of conservative leaders. Just as we expect better
from our children, we should be able to expect more from these mean-
spirited and idiotic American leaders.

THIRTEEN

Without Hope, Blacks and Latinas/os Will Take to the Streets

Dr. Alvaro Huerta

While millions of Americans have suddenly become enlightened about the bleak plight of racial minorities in segregated inner-cities and impoverished suburbs, especially with the spate of police killings of unarmed blacks, for those of us who grew up in America's ghettoes and barrios, we are all too familiar with the rampant cases of police misconduct and government negligence.

As police chiefs, commissioners, prosecutors, politicians and media reporters commonly portray police killings of unarmed racialized minorities as isolated cases, where the cases through self-serving inquiries by the same departments that employ the responsible parties, how much longer must historically disenfranchised and racialized groups wait before justice is served? For people of color, when examining the unacceptable police killings (and high incarceration rates) of blacks and Latinas/os in America, there's no "justice" — there's only "just us."

In this country, we are taught from a young age that we must be responsible for our actions and pay the consequences, when we do something wrong. Thus, when no one is held accountable for the deadly and abusive behavior by the same people enlisted to "protect and to serve" us, there comes to a boiling point where those on the receiving end of the abuse must demand to be heard on the streets. Police abuse and street riots or protests by impacted communities of color repeat themselves throughout American history. Before the 2015 protests in Baltimore, for instance, we had the Watts Riots in 1965. Before Ferguson blew up in 2014, we had the Los Angeles Riots in 1992. Contrary to mainstream interpretations by media outlets and elected officials, riots or protests represent collective expressions of despair and hopelessness found in disenfranchised and racialized communities that push blacks and Latinas/os to release their frustration on the streets. Thus, let's not victimize the victims by blaming the protestors!

While it's politically convenient and too simplistic for mainstream media outlets and elected officials to scapegoat the victims of police abuse, racial segregation and government neglect by referring to Baltimore protestors as "thugs" and "criminals"—where even Baltimore Mayor Stephanie Rawlings-Blake and President Barack Obama, as African Americans and Democrats, used similar language—it's politically inconvenient and more nuanced to examine the root causes leading to these disturbances, such as institutional racism, police abuse and, more broadly, capitalism.

Why don't those in power use these same pejorative terms, "thugs" and "criminals," when describing the civic leaders, politicians, government officials and business leaders who have historically played a major role in creating impoverished ghettos and barrios through racist polices, anti-worker actions and government neglect? More specifically, what's more thuggish and criminal than race restrictive covenants, redlining, residential segregation, dysfunctional public schools, urban renewal, white flight to the suburbs and the exportation of manufacturing jobs to foreign countries?

The bleak plight of blacks and Latinas/os is both professional and personal for me. Long before I received my graduate degrees and became a professor, where I study cities and the disenfranchised individuals/ families who inhabit them, I was raised in East Los Angeles' notorious Ramona Gardens housing project.

Like many of my childhood friends, I was well aware that two gangs ruled the projects: the dominant gang (Big Hazard) and the police (LAPD). While I never joined the gang—not because I felt morally superior, but because I lacked the necessary physical attributes to fight—I never experienced abuse or pressure from the homeboys to join. (I commonly joke that my gang application was "rejected," since I was too thin to defend the barrio.) This is mainly because we all grew up together, attended the same elementary school and played street sports as kids. As we grew older, we took different paths without any conflict.

However, as for the police or cops, I only experienced negative encounters. Growing up, in the eyes of the cops (and housing authority officials), it was clear to me that we—poor kids from the projects—all looked alike and were up to no good. For example, as a sixteen-year-old, I was pulled over while teaching myself how to drive. Viewing me as a threat, one of the cops pulled out his gun and pointed it toward me. What was my crime? I was making a rolling stop.

While I became accustomed to being pulled over, frisked and questioned by the cops in the projects, I never expected this harassment to follow me to UCLA, when I first enrolled as a freshman (majoring in mathematics) in 1985. Call me naïve, but I initially thought that by being one of the few Chicanas/os from the projects to pursue higher education, when most of my childhood friends were dropping out of high school (or being pushed out), serving time in jail and working dead-end jobs, I would escape police harassment. Instead, as a seventeen-year-old, I was pulled over by the cops near the Westwood campus. I learned the hard way that racism would follow me from the Eastside to the Westside. I also learned that racism will always be a part of my life with or without university degrees.

Moving forward, American leaders must stop blaming the victims of an unequal, racist and capitalist society, where elective officials, government officials and business leaders seek superficial remedies for so-called isolated incidents, such as police abuse. Instead, we must tackle the structural causes of inequality and institutional racism to create a more just and equal society for all.

FOURTEEN
El Robo

In Memory of My Mexican Mother

Dr. Alvaro Huerta

Carmen Mejia was the prettiest girl in her *rancho, Sajo Grande*—located in the beautiful state of Michoacán, Mexico. As a thirteen-year-old girl with the sparkling green eyes, she already had a boyfriend, an admirer and a stalker.

In the 1950s, rural Mexico was not the safest place for unwed girls, where some men would abduct teenage girls with the aim of eventually marrying them. Once taken from her home for several nights, an abducted girl had no choice but to marry her abductor to protect her honor and family name.

Carmen rarely spoke with Alfredo Ramirez, the boyfriend. They only met a few times, under the close supervision of Carmen's mother, who watched their every move from a close distance. Carmen and Alfredo never went on dates, kissed or held hands. He was okay with their non-physical relationship, especially since he felt honored that Carmen selected him over the others in the *rancho* who only dreamed of courting her.

Salomon Chavez Huerta, the admirer, also had his eyes on Carmen. Belonging to a large and respected family, this handsome young man could wed any girl he pursued. However, he had already set his eyes on Carmen and nobody could change his mind. It was only a matter of time when he would make his move.

Alcadio Perez, the stalker, was not so patient. What he lacked in good looks, he compensated with obsession and determination. It was no secret that he wanted to make Carmen his wife, at any cost.

While Alfredo played the role of the gentleman and Salomon the confident one, Alcadio behaved like a brute. As a brute, Alcadio never sent Carmen flowers or love notes. He had a simpler plan. He would stalk Carmen, seeking his opportunity to abduct her.

Once he crafted his master plan, Alcadio and his hired thugs stationed themselves inside the cornfields, adjacent to Carmen's home. After hiding for days with only uncooked corn to eat and mescal to drink, Alcadio and his posse made their move.

"The old man left the house for the day," Alcadio whispered to his accomplices.

"Let's wait for her to go outside," one of the thugs responded.

"Sounds good to me," stated the other one.

A few hours later, Carmen ventured outside her adobe home with an empty bucket to get water from her neighbor, Margarita.

"There she is," Alcadio whispered to the others. "I don't see the old lady. She must be cooking inside."

Oblivious of the pursuing stalkers, Carmen skipped her way to Margarita's house.

Suddenly, Alcadio ran toward Carmen and grabbed her.

"Let me go!" Carmen screamed at the top of her lungs, while Alcadio and his fellow brutes grabbed her by the arms and legs.

"Shut up!" Alcadio responded. "Your father is not here to protect you."

"Somebody help!" Carmen yelled to her neighbors, who began to gather in a semi-circle to witness all of the commotion.

"Let her go, Alcadio!" a young woman yelled from the crowd.

"Yeah," stated an older woman. "You can't take her. She doesn't belong to you!"

"I'm going to tell your mother that you're involved," Carmen's best friend, Rosa, told one of the thugs, who also happened to be his second cousin.

Fearful of the growing crowd, the hired thugs fled the scene.

"Don't go," Alcadio pleaded with them to stay and help. "I'll throw in an extra 500 *pesos*."

Carmen then broke free and headed directly to her house.

Not willing to give up just yet, Alcadio grabbed Carmen from her long, braided hair, forcing her to the ground before reaching her house. Carmen desperately picked up a rock from the ground and, without looking, hit Alcadio on his forehead. He started to bleed profusely.

Freed from his savage grip, Carmen made her way home. Blinded by the blood, Alcadio couldn't catch up to Carmen.

Alcadio then reached for his silver revolver.

"If I can't have you, nobody can," Alcadio screamed, aimlessly shooting his gun at Carmen.

Carmen miraculously made it inside her home without a bullet wound. Alcadio quickly fled the scene before the local militia arrived. As he retreated to the hills, Alcadio held a lock of Carmen's long hair in his hand, bringing a sinister smile to his otherwise bloody face.

Once Salomon learned of the almost deadly incident, he wasted no time in asking Carmen to be his girlfriend, especially since Alfredo, who left to *el norte* for work, couldn't protect her from Alcadio and other brutes like him. Seeking justice, Salomon sought help from his father, Martin. As the commander of the local militia, Martin had the authority to arrest Alcadio and his men.

Witnesses told Martin that Alcadio headed north, yet the militia commander decided to head south in pursuit of Alcadio. Carmen later learned that Martin had no intention of capturing Alcadio, since the brute's father just happened to be Martin's first cousin.

Salomon realized that Alcadio paid off his neighbor Raul to distract Salomon while the stalker executed his foiled master plan.

"How could you betray me?" asked Salomon, while pistol-whipping Raul.

"That's enough!" said Martin, ordering his son to stop.

"Okay," responded Salomon. "Now, let's get that bastard, Alcadio."

"Don't worry about Alcadio," said Martin. "He failed. He won't be coming around the *rancho* anymore, especially now that you and Carmen are together. Now, let's plan that wedding."

Fortunately for my seven siblings and me, my mother, Carmen, eventually married my father, Salomon.

Throughout her life in Mexico and the United States, my mother overcame tremendous obstacles to make sure that her eight children enjoyed a better life than hers to get ahead. Now, if only she could be alive, just one more day, so she could tell me her favorite story of how she triumphed against her would-be abductor in the *rancho*.

FIFTEEN

La Pistola

In Memory of My Mexican Father

Dr. Alvaro Huerta

My father, Salomon Chavez Huerta, never left home without his gun. It was a sleek .38-Special revolver, which he hid in his left cowboy boot whenever he took a walk in our violent barrio in East Los Angeles.

My father grew up on a small Mexican *rancho*, *Sajo Grande*, in the beautiful state Michoacán, where rural communities are known for their bloody family feuds—similar to America's famous McCoy-Hatfield feud in Appalachia. As the oldest male of ten siblings, he led the family rivalry during the 1950s. It took the lives of numerous family members on both sides and forced many to flee to *el norte*.

After losing his brother, Pascual, to the bloody feud, most of the Huerta clan moved to Tijuana in Baja California, Mexico. My extended family later migrated to Los Angeles—Hollywood to be more specific. We lived in a three story Craftsman house with too many siblings, cousins, aunts and uncles at any given time to count. Seeking more privacy, my immediate family of ten moved to East Los Angeles. Little did my parents know that they relocated the family from one violent place, *Sajo Grande*, to another one, Ramona Gardens housing project (or Big Hazard projects).

When we first moved into the projects, my older brother Salomon and me didn't leave our apartment for two weeks for fear of the unknown. Once we did, a local posse of kids awaited us. Tomas, the leader, arranged for us to fight two other neighborhood kids. Unlike affluent suburban communities, for the newcomer kids, it was a traditional welcome to fight to show our toughness. Fortunately, my brother and me had some Bruce Lee martial arts moves up our sleeves. We learned martial arts by watching movies like *Enter the Dragon, Game of Death* and *Fist of Fury.*

One summer morning, several years later, Tomas and Fat Johnny decided to swing my brother from his arms and legs. Not knowing that they were playing, my father quickly ran outside to save his son from the bullies. As he pushed Tomas away, Tomas' mother attacked my father from behind. Like a Mexican *luchador*, my father slammed her to the ground and fled the scene with my brother.

Later that evening, my father got word that Tomas' older brother, Chuco—a respected gang leader who had done time in Folsom for attempted murder—was looking for him to take revenge.

Unable to locate my older brother, my father summoned me to his room.

"Alvaro, I need to talk to you," he said in his typical stoic demeanor.

"Okay," I said, wondering what I did wrong.

"Here, take my gun," he said casually. "Put it under your belt in your backside. I want you to come outside with me. I need to talk to Chuco."

It was cold that night, as my father and me walked around our brick building a couple of times, looking for Chuco. My knees began to shake and my heart pounded, as we approached a bunch of older homeboys or *veteranos* who were drinking a twenty-four-pack of Budweiser.

"That's them," my father said.

"I think we should call the cops," I said innocently, not yet mastering rules of the projects: never rat!

"What for?" he told me. "Don't you know that the cops are just another gang."

My father walked straight to the homeboys. He was holding a small, paper bag with an object in it.

"Chuco, is that you?" he asked someone from the group of homeboys.

"What is it, old man?" came a voice from the darkness.

"Can I talk to you?" my father said.

"There's nothing to talk about," said Chuco. "I already know the whole story."

My father slowly reached into the paper bag.

"You better step back or else," Chuco said, putting his hands in his Pendleton coat pockets.

Instead of reaching for my father's gun, I froze and brazed for the worst. "It would be nice to have clear instructions from my father!" I thought to myself in a mini-panic.

Undeterred by Chuco's threat, my father pulled out a bottle of Jose Cuervo Tequila (Especial Gold) that he purchased on his regular *mandados* to Tijuana. (Apart from the tequila, he never failed to bring us delicious *pan dulce*.)

Slowly, as homeboys usually operate, Chuco took his hands out from his pockets and reached for the bottle.

"You have a lot of guts, old man," he said, giving my father an *abrazo*.

"I hope everything is fine between us," my father responded in Spanish for reassurance.

"Everything's cool," said Chuco. "You could've called the cops, but you approached me like a man, so I'm going to forget about everything that happened and give you a pass."

Relieved, my father looked at me, where I was still shaken up.

He then said to me, "Let's go home before we miss the *Bonanza* re-run on television."

As tears rolled down my face, I smiled.

SIXTEEN

Lessons My Mexican Father Taught Me

Dr. Alvaro Huerta

When I hear about American leaders scapegoating Latina/o immigrants, I can't help but think about my late father, Salomon Chavez Huerta. Like millions of other immigrants in this country, my father endured a harsh life in Mexico and sacrificed greatly to settle a family in the United States. While he was a stoic man, before succumbing to cancer at sixty-seven years old, he labored on both sides of the border, toiling as a farmworker, factory janitor and day laborer.

Born on March 9, 1930, in *Sajo Grande*—a small *rancho* in the beautiful state of Michoacán, Mexico—my father and his immediate family grew up in a place with no indoor plumbing, hot water, electricity, telephones or paved roads. Lacking formal education, at a very young age, he joined his brothers and father in working the land to grow corn and raise livestock. Like millions of their *paisanos*, they worked from sun-up to sundown.

He first migrated to the United States as a young man, working as a farmworker during the Bracero Program—the U.S.-Mexico guest worker program of the mid-twentieth century. While my father appreciated the opportunity to work as a *bracero* to support his family in his *rancho* or hometown, he experienced severe cases of abuse and humiliation. This included the brutal intake process (e.g., being sprayed with the cancer-causing chemical DDT), substandard living circumstances and inhumane working conditions.

There are many reasons why Mexicans migrate to *el norte*. In my father's case, it wasn't simply to pursue higher wages. It was also to

65

escape the violence that plagued his hometown. Just like the famous American Hatfield-McCoy blood feud in Appalachia during the late nineteenth century, my father and uncles became embroiled in a deadly feud with a rival family.

In his attempt to flee a violent environment, my father, along with his extended family, migrated to Tijuana (Baja California, Mexico). Eventually, after spending a couple of years in Hollywood, California, my immediate family moved and settled in East Los Angeles.

Lacking formal education and basic English skills, my father worked as a janitor in a factory, producing aluminum alloy wheels. Making a measly $3.25 per hour for more than a decade, one day—when demanded by his white supervisor to work in the furnace—he had enough and quit in protest. After doing the math, he realized that he could "bring in more money" by collecting public assistance or welfare, instead of resorting to another underpaid, dead-end job. While he tried to rationalize his limited choices, the truth can't be denied: the system broke him.

Instead of going to work, he spent most of his time visiting family in Tijuana, running errands or *mandados* and watching television. He loved to watch Westerns, such as re-runs of *Bonanza* and *The Rifleman*. He also loved Clint Eastwood movies, like *The Good, the Bad and the Ugly* and *The Outlaw Josey Wales*. Since my father rarely engaged in small talk, if I wanted to bond with him, I had to join him on our old, red sofa—covered in sticky plastic—sitting and watching his favorite television programs. These programs took him back to a simpler time in his past, one that, albeit violent, he could relate to.

One day, my mother—who always encouraged my siblings and me to pursue higher education—told my father to turn off the television for one Saturday so he take my older brother and me to the Westside to work as a day laborer. While I had always excelled in mathematics and, overall, done well in school, as a thirteen-year-old, I was too lazy to perform physical housework or yard work. Waking up late on weekends, I was just a typical American teen. This also applied to my older brother, Salomon. Concerned about our laziness, my mother convinced my father to teach my brother and me a lesson on how difficult it is to survive as low-wage laborers and to appreciate the educational opportunities available in this country.

Not wasting any time, the following Saturday morning, my father woke up my brother and me at 5:00 a.m. to get ready for work. I'd never been up so early and, for a moment, I thought that the world was about to end. After getting ready and taking a two-hour bus ride, we reached a busy street corner in Malibu.

Surrounded by Mexican immigrant men jostling to get the attention of mostly privileged white men in their luxury cars (e.g., Mercedes, BMW and Jaguar), my father quickly joined the fray for a day job. As I watched from the sidelines, I noticed my father running to get the attention of a white man in a black Porsche 911.

For the first time in my life, I was ashamed of my father. I was not used to seeing a grown man, especially my stoic father, "running and begging for work." Many years later, I realized that I was wrong to be ashamed. Instead, I should have been thankful for my father's (and mother's) efforts to teach my brother and me a hard lesson about the pitfalls of manual labor.

Once I secured my graduate university degrees from UCLA and UC Berkeley—with the unconditional support of my wife Antonia—I had exceeded my mother's dream for me to pursue my bachelor's degree. (This applies to my brother Salomon who earned his MFA from UCLA.) Yet, despite all of my academic successes, which includes winning fellowships/awards, securing a faculty position and publishing books/articles, I will never forget that Saturday morning when my father—a poor Mexican immigrant from a small *rancho* with no formal education— taught me two valuable lessons that I've never learned in the Ivory Tower: there's no shame in manual labor and it's noble to sacrifice for others.

That's what millions of my Mexican immigrants do on a daily basis in the United States.

Over twenty years after his death, I will never forgive myself for not telling my father how I felt about him: "I'm so proud to be your son."

SEVENTEEN

The Day My Mexican Father Met Cesar Chavez

Dr. Alvaro Huerta

My father, Salomon Chavez Huerta, first arrived in this country as an agricultural worker during the Bracero Program—the U.S.-Mexico guest worker program of the mid-twentieth century. This important program met this country's dire labor shortages not only in the agricultural fields during two major wars (WWII and Korean War), but also in key transportation sectors, like railroads. Despite their major contributions, Mexican immigrants, confronted racism and work-place abuse from the dominant culture, where they experienced poor wages, residential segregation and limited upward mobility opportunities.

It wasn't until my graduate studies that I learned more in detail about what the *braceros*—as honest, hardworking men—experienced and sacrificed during this exploitative labor program. While receiving meager wages for physically demanding work, the American and Mexican administrations, along with affiliated banks, deducted ten percent from their wages, as part of a so-called savings program. The *braceros* never received the money owed to them. It took a successful class-action lawsuit, filed in California in 2001, for some of these men to receive long overdue compensation. However, many of them, like my father, had died by then without receiving monies owed to them.

I also learned other facts about this program that provided me with some insight about what my father and millions of his *paisanos* experienced, which made many of them reluctant to speak in detail to their children and grandchildren about their harsh days as *braceros*. As part of the screening process in Mexico, for example, these proud Mexican men went through central processing centers. At these centers, U.S. Department of Agriculture personnel forced them to strip naked in large rooms (without any privacy), spraying them with DDT—a powerful insecticide linked to cancer and reproductive health ailments. During this period, the photojournalist Leonard Nadel did an excellent job of documenting these humiliating experiences, including the terrible housing and working conditions.

My involvement in social justice causes prompted my father to open up more about his days as a *bracero*. Many years ago, while protesting the then-Immigration & Naturalization Service (INS) and its inhumane practices of detaining/imprisoning entire families in chained-up hotels and motels in Los Angeles, I appeared on a local Spanish-language news program. My uncle Javier told my father that I was on television. For someone who lacked formal education, from a small *rancho* in Michoacán, Mexico, it was a big deal for his son to be on television, like a famous actor in a Mexican *telenovela*.

Inspired by my social activism, my father told me a story about the time he met Cesar Chavez—co-founder of the United Farmworkers Union (UFW) with Dolores Huerta. Actually, it was shortly after the Bracero Program ended, when my father, like many other *braceros*, returned to the U.S. to work in the agricultural fields—both with and without work permits. In fact, as documented by Princeton's Dr. Douglas S. Massey and other immigration scholars, this guest worker program played a major role for millions of Mexicans to eventually settle in this country.

In 1965, while my father was working in Delano, California, a group of Mexican farmworkers, including Filipinos, launched the historic grape boycott. As the farmworker leaders were recruiting potential members to join the union's efforts and boycott, one of them assembled a group of men after their work shift. The other organizers provided the farmworkers with name tags.

"I didn't know who he was, but he introduced himself as Cesar," my father told me.

"Did you talk to him?" I asked.

"No, but he made it a point to learn everyone's name, shake their hands and ask them to join the boycott," he said.

"And then what happened?" I responded, hoping that my father would tell me a fantastic story about him being the unheralded leader of the grape boycott. (While attending UCLA, I guess I had taken too many Chicana/o classes with the eminent historian, Dr. Juan Gómez-Quiñones.)

"He got close to me, looked at my name on my shirt and smiled," he said, building suspense to his story.

"And then what happened?" I asked, again, wondering how the story would end.

"Look at your name tag," my father proudly recollected Cesar Chavez telling him, "your middle name 'Chavez' is like my last name and your last name 'Huerta' is like Dolores' last name."

Now that's a story!

EIGHTEEN

A Chicana/o Love Story

Tribute to a Wise and Beautiful Chicana

Dr. Alvaro Huerta

When it came to girls, as a teenager, I was shy. It wasn't that I feared that they would beat me up, like the bullies I evaded on the mean streets of East Los Angeles; I simply feared rejection.

For some mysterious reason that I still don't understand, I felt that if I got rejected, all of my friends and complete strangers would somehow find out and make fun of me for eternity. I didn't want to be that "reject" or "loser" teen. Life was difficult enough, trying to survive in the Ramona Gardens housing project (or Big Hazard projects). It didn't help that I was thin, while growing up in a tough neighborhood. This helps explain why I never joined the local gang, since I worried that my gang "application" would be rejected, especially since I couldn't defend the neighborhood.

Once I arrived at UCLA as a freshman (majoring in mathematics), my entire world changed. Being one of the few working-class Chicanas/os on campus, I quickly became a student activist. I began to break out of my shyness. From advocating for immigrant rights to demanding more racialized minorities in higher education, I became articulate, passionate and bold. While I became a member of the main Chicana/o student group—*Movimiento Estudiantil Chicano de Aztlán* (MEChA)—by my sophomore year, I was co-chair of the Chicano Education Project (ChEP), where we mentored and motivated Chicana/o students in public high schools to pursue higher education.

I will never forget that one ChEP meeting when a beautiful Chicana, Antonia, joined us for the first time. She was a first-year student from the

73

Westside and had it all: good looks, smarts and commitment to social change. Later, I found out that our parents had strikingly similar backgrounds. While both of our Mexican mothers worked as domestic workers, our Mexican fathers first arrived in the U.S. as agricultural workers under the Bracero Program—the U.S.-Mexico guest worker program of the mid-twentieth century.

I initially thought that Antonia was out of my league. But with my new sense of confidence—thanks to my student activism—I was no longer that math nerd in high school who perpetually found himself in the dreaded "friend zone" with girls. I decided I just needed to be strategic in my approach, especially since I had fierce competition on campus for Antonia's attention.

Utilizing my new political skills, I developed a master plan. Before asking out Antonia for a date, I approached my competitors—or "predators," as I fondly recall them—and told them of my intentions. For those who didn't respect my request—actually, it was more like a demand or threat—I had no option but to undermine them with Antonia. Once I did away with the competition, I worked up the nerve to ask her out.

"It's not like I want to be your boyfriend or anything like that, but do you want to go eat somewhere at Westwood since my financial aid just arrived?" I recall asking her.

"Sure," she said.

It appeared that my new political skills were working. Well, it was more like "innocent stalking," since I "coincidentally" registered for the same classes she was taking. I also "accidentally" visited her dorm on more than one occasion.

On one such occasion she asked, "What are you doing at Sproul Hall?"

"I'm recruiting for ChEP members to visit San Fernando High School," I said, without missing a beat. (It helps when you stay up all night thinking about the different responses to potential questions, just like preparing for a college debate.)

After spending more time together, I decided to take the next step.

"It's not like I want to marry you or anything, but do you want to be my girlfriend?" I asked.

"If I say 'yes,' will you promise to stop being my 'friendly' stalker?" she joked.

We kissed in my blue VW Beetle, where I said, "I'm in Disneyland."

I'm just glad that nobody from my old neighborhood overheard me. My street cred from the projects would've withered away.

After leaving the university, we continued seeing each other. Eventually, I popped the big question.

"Will you marry me?" I asked, with even more confidence.

"Yes!" she exclaimed.

Many moons later, I only hope that our son, Joaquin, will have my same luck to meet a wise and beautiful Chicana to fall in love with.

NINETEEN

Trump's Racist Comments Help Democrats in the Future

Dr. Alvarao Huerta

As a scholar of Mexican heritage, I was appalled, but not surprised, by television personality Donald J. Trump's racist comments against Mexican immigrants on June 16, 2015. In announcing his bid for the White House, Trump didn't mince his words when he vulgarly uttered: "When Mexico sends its people, they're not sending their best. They're not sending you . . . They're sending people that have lots of problems, and they're bringing those problems with us. They're bringing drugs. They're bringing crime. They're rapists . . . " (Lee, *The Washington Post*).

I will not try to counter these racist and baseless comments. To do so, I will fall into the trap that Trump sets up — like the provocateur extraordinaire and racist commentator Ann Coulter — where he purposely makes outrageous comments for people to respond to in order to promote his self-interest. It's not about logic or reason with Trump. It's about branding and self-marketing. For Trump, there's no such thing as bad publicity. There's no end to his narcissism.

While one can easily view Trump's or Coulter's xenophobic comments as simple-minded or idiotic, let's not forget that we're not talking about non-educated individuals. They both have Ivy League degrees. By dismissing them as "dimwits" — very tempting, I must admit! — many critics ignore their ulterior motives. When they make ridiculous or bombastic comments, Trump and Coulter know exactly what they're doing. They're generating national news to sell their products — free of cost.

By reaching millions of Americans via social media, mainstream media outlets and news programs, Trump and Coulter — similar to the Kar-

77

dashians—have an uncanny ability to monopolize what Americans think and talk about. They say and do things that millions of Americans, particularly white folks, would only utter in the privacy of their homes. Also, many Americans pay attention to them, like the popular radio personality Howard Stern, for one simple fact: the shock value.

Since he's entered the crowded Republican nomination race for president, Trump has become a major liability for the GOP. By making racist comments and feuding with reporter Jorge Ramos (the influential Spanish-language network Univision), among other key Latinas/os and groups, Trump has taken the spotlight away from his fellow Republican candidates. Instead of attacking presidential candidate Hilary Clinton on her policies, Republican candidates—including Jeb Bush, Chris Christy, Marco Rubio, Ted Cruz, Carly Fiorina, Scott Walker and Rand Paul, along with the growing list of Republicans—have been relegated to spectators of "The Trump Show." Given that a major television network like NBC recently joined Univision in pulling the plug on Trump's Miss Universe pageant, it's only a matter of time when Trump feels additional financial consequences from his racist comments, such as loss of business from Macy's and Serta, along with other companies who have and will cut business ties with him.

Politically, Trump's racist comments will not only tarnish his image among the millions of Latinas/os in this country, especially those of Mexican descent, but these racist words will also continue to hurt the already damaged Republican brand among this country's largest racialized group and others. This is a lesson that former Republican presidential nominee Mitt Romney learned the hard way when he articulated his plan for America's 11 million undocumented immigrants living in the shadows: self-deport.

Apart from Latinas/os, Republicans will continue to alienate other important voting blocs, like Asian and Pacific Islanders, where immigration remains a popular issue. Also, given that Republican leaders haven't adequately condemned Trump's racist comments, the GOP's weak response speaks volumes to Latinas/os. In addition, since Mexico represents a friendly neighbor and huge trading partner with the U.S., Trump's derogatory comments against Mexicans will rightly cement anti-American sentiments throughout Latin America. On a popular level, Mexicans quickly responded with their humor and creativity: a Trump piñata!

In the case of the Democrats, if they want to win the White House in future elections, they should not only condemn Trump's racist comments, but also advance a political agenda that's diverse and progressive to advance the basic needs of Latinas/os and other racialized groups in this country.

TWENTY

New Republican Xenophobic Policies Will Inevitably Backfire

Dr. Alvaro Huerta

In the wake of the tragic murder of Kathryn Steinle in San Francisco, California, Republican leaders in Congress shamefully introduce new anti-immigration bills. Instead of offering their condolences and mourning the death of Steinle on July 1, 2015, allegedly by Francisco Sanchez, a released undocumented immigrant from San Francisco County Jail, Republicans in the Senate and House exploited this senseless crime with draconian immigration measures.

On July 23, 2015, led by Rep. Duncan D. Hunter (R-CA), the House approved a bill by a 241–175 margin, mainly on party lines, to financially punish sanctuary cities, like San Francisco. Essentially, sanctuary cities represent municipalities that don't inquire into the legal status of detained individuals and don't coordinate with U.S. Immigration and Customs Enforcement (ICE) to enforce inhumane immigration laws under the jurisdiction of the federal government. In sanctuary cities, for instance, police and jail authorities don't comply with ICE detainer requests to hold and transfer over an apprehended undocumented immigrant.

Should this bill eventually prevail in the Senate, President Barack Obama signaled that he would veto it since it ignores comprehensive immigration reforms. Given that this draconian bill conveniently ignores the racial profiling of Latinas/os under ICE detainer requests and fosters distrust among immigrants with local authorities, Republican leaders have pushed other harsh measures targeting immigrants. Over a week after Kathryn's killing, Rep. Matt Salmon (R-AZ) introduced H.R. 3004 or

"Kate's Law" in the House, where deported immigrants who re-enter the country will serve five-year, minimum prison sentences. In a time when the United States leads the world in jailing its population, especially African Americans and Latinas/os, Republicans want to incarcerate more brown bodies at a high financial and moral price.

Not satisfied with these inhumane bills, Sen. Charles Grassley (R-IA) introduced legislation in the Senate that includes the punitive measures against sanctuary cities and "Kate's Law." The only "comprehensive" aspect about this legislation is its attack on Latinas/os. For many Latinas/os, there's no separation between being "undocumented" versus "documented." Being family-oriented, many Latinas/os view legislative attacks against undocumented immigrants as attacks against them.

In Latina/o communities, undocumented immigrants are not strangers; they are not marginal or isolated individuals. They are our parents, brothers, sisters, cousins, uncles and grandparents. They are our *compadres, comadres, padrinos* and *madrinas*. They are our neighbors and co-workers. They are integrated members of our communities. In short, they are *familia*. This explains why immigration represents a key issue for Latinas/os, apart from jobs, healthcare and education.

Given the importance of the Latina/o vote, Democratic leaders wasted no time in referring to the anti-sanctuary city legislation as the "Donald Trump Act." While Republicans remain mean-spirited and short-sighted in their anti-immigration legislative agenda, Democrats should embrace, without compromise, the browning of America.

In the short-term, if Republican leaders don't recognize the dramatic demographic changes occurring in this country and the importance of the Latina/o vote, in the long-term, they will be doomed.

TWENTY-ONE

Trump Exemplifies
True Colors of GOP

Dr. Alvaro Huerta

It's not true that Republican presidential candidate Donald Trump only represents the extreme wing or "crazies" of the GOP. As a leader in numerous political polls, Trump exemplifies the true colors of the GOP: xenophobic, racist and mean-spirited. Despite how the other GOP presidential candidates or Republican leaders view him or distance themselves from his vitriolic language, Trump's boorish behavior and racist disdain toward Latina/o immigrants represents the Republican party's political platform. While Republican leaders have acknowledged that it's impossible or not feasible to deport over 11 million undocumented immigrants, they have rejected a pathway to citizenship for those who live and work in America's shadows. In lieu of citizenship, Republican leaders propose a form of legal status without the opportunity for citizenship. Essentially, they argue for a legalized, second-class pool of workers available for "cheap" and exploitable labor.

What does it matter for millions of Latina/o immigrants if Trump refers to them in pejorative terms, when more diplomatic Republican leaders, like former Florida Gov. Jed Bush, concur that citizenship is not an option for those who toil from sun-up to sun-down in our households, front yards, agricultural fields, kitchens, factories, hospitals and office buildings?

This is shameful!

As a Chicano scholar, I'm not simply concerned about Trump using racist rhetoric toward Mexicans immigrants—which does matter. But, fundamentally, I'm more concerned about his reactionary policies and racist programs that negatively impact Latina/o immigrants in particular and Latinas/os in general. More specifically, Trump's reactionary policies and racist programs foster the same deplorable outcomes for marginalized Latinas/os and African Americans that Republicans (and Democrats) have been peddling for decades: residential segregation, poor public schools, low-paying jobs, lack of quality jobs, police violence, high incarceration rates, lack of access to higher education and diminished upward mobility opportunities.

By viciously attacking Latina/o immigrants, Trump makes it crystal clear to Latinas/os and other racialized groups that they are not welcomed in the GOP. As for the minority of Latina/o Republicans, they represent tokens and sell-outs in a political party that has no interest in meeting the basic needs of people who look like them. For example, given that Latinas/os benefit tremendously from the Affordable Care Act (or Obamacare), before seeking to spend billions on the U.S.-Mexico border and other foolish expenditures, Republican policies will continue to harm Latinas/os.

Trump is not alone in his racist and immoral behavior, however. On a recent campaign tour in Iowa, Wisconsin Governor Scott Walker hectored two distraught children of an undocumented immigrant about the rule of law. When the children asked Walker if he wanted to deport their father, who would benefit from President Barack Obama's immigration executive order, Deferred Action for Parents of Americans (DAPA), Walker offered them a cold-blooded lecture. If Walker and fellow Republican leaders care so much about the rule of law, where were they when then-President George W. Bush invaded Iraq under false pretenses? Where was the GOP when Bush sanctioned torture, such as waterboarding? And why are Republican leaders silent when the police unlawfully kill unarmed African Americans and Latinas/os on a regular basis?

Apart from being mean-spirited and hypocritical, Republic leaders continue to advocate for policies that benefit rich people and corporations. By proposing tax-breaks for the rich and allowing for corporations to avoid paying their fair share of taxes, Republicans engage in class warfare against working-class Latinas/os. By following what then-President Ronald Reagan made famous with "Reaganomics" or "trickle-down economics," under the false assumption that tax breaks for the rich will ultimately "trickle-down" to benefit the working-class, there's only one thing that trickles down to working-class Latinas/os under this absurd policy: misery.

As Trump continues to lead in state and national polls, where Republicans seek to retake the White House, win or lose, the GOP, as a major political power, will gradually wither away.

"Carmen Mejia Huerta" by Salomon Huerta, 2005

"Salomon Chavez Huerta" by Salomon Huerta, 2019

Salomon Huerta on left and author on right, Tijuana, Baja California, Mexico by Catalina Huerta, circa 1970

Hazard graffiti in the Ramona Gardens housing project by Pablo Aguilar, 2005

"Los Tres Caballeros" by Salomon Huerta, 1992

"Untitled" kid being shot charcoal by Salomon Huerta, 1991

Author in front of a mural in the Ramona Gardens housing project by Pablo Aguilar, 2005

"La Pistola" by Salomon Huerta, 2017

Author, Salomon Huerta, Noel Huerta, and Ismael Huerta in the Ramona Gardens housing project by Pablo Aguilar, 2005

In Memory of Noel "Nene" Huerta by Salomon Huerta, 2017

"*Abajo con la migra*" by Andrew Huerta, 2017

Author on right with Latino gardeners by Ed Carreón, 2009

"Antonia Montes" by Salomon Huerta, 1994

"Frida Kahlo" by Salomon Huerta, 2017

"Dolores Huerta" by Salomon Huerta, 2017

"Dr. Juan Gómez-Quiñones" by Salomon Huerta, 2017

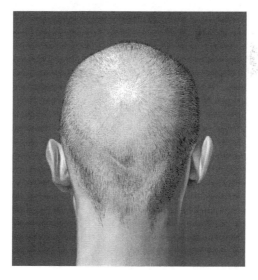

"Untitled" back of the head painting by Salomon Huerta, 1999

"Untitled" Mexican *luchador* painting by Salomon Huerta, 2008

TWENTY-TWO

Trump's Mass Deportation Plan Symbolizes White Privilege

Dr. Alvaro Huerta

Donald Trump, the leading Republican candidate in the GOP primary, has a strange way of expressing his so-called "love" for Latinas/os. After generalizing Mexican immigrants as "drug dealers," "criminals" and "rapists" on June 16, 2015, later that month, in a Virginia golf course, he bizarrely uttered, "Latinos love Trump and I love them" (Schwartz, Real Clear Politics). To paraphrase the popular saying, with friends like Trump, who needs enemies?

Two months later, Trump doubled down on his nativist slurs/positions against Latina/o immigrants. On his official website for president, along with an interview on NBC's "Meet the Press" with Chuck Todd, Trump elaborated on his extremist views toward one of the most vulnerable groups in this country: undocumented immigrants. While many of his fellow Republican candidates for president supported some form of second-class "legal status" for the estimated 11 million undocumented immigrants in the U.S., which is also not accessible, Trump mercilessly argues for the mass deportation of all of undocumented immigrants. The cost of detaining, processing and deporting all undocumented immigrants, according to several experts, falls between $100 billion to $200 billion. This doesn't include hundreds of billions of dollars for future enforcement measures. Does this make Trump a fiscal conservative, as he claims to be?

This inhumane and preposterous position, which should be condemned by all presidential candidates, including President Barack Obama, is popular among Republican voters. According to a recent poll conducted by CNN-ORC, 63 percent of Republicans agree with Trump in deporting all undocumented immigrants (Zurcher, BBC News). If Republican leaders believe that they can gain a significant portion of the Latina/o vote in future elections with their leading candidate and large portion of their members in support of hostile language and political positions against Latina/o immigrants, they will surely experience a rude awaking.

In 2012, for example, Republican presidential candidate Mitt Romney and his "self-deport" immigration policy garnered him only low 27 percent of the Latina/o vote and a mere 26 percent of the Asian American vote. This is not a winning formula in appealing to these key voting blocs.

As part of his racist campaign, Trump also proposes to deport undocumented immigrants as family units. This includes mixed families, where some members are undocumented and others are documented. Trump also aims to eliminate President Obama's executive order for undocumented immigrant youth, Deferred Action for Childhood Arrivals (DACA). These youth are usually referred to as DREAMers.

Adding insult to injury, Trump proposes to strip citizenship from U.S.-born children of undocumented immigrants. In this particular case, Trump plans to change the Constitution, specifically the Fourteenth Amendment, which stipulations the following: "All persons born or naturalized in the United States, and subject to the jurisdiction thereof, are citizens of the United States and of the State wherein they reside."

Someone in Congress needs to teach Trump about the complexities of changing the Constitution! Changing or amending the Constitution is not the same or as easy as making a financial payment to porn star or Playboy Playmate. Trump's xenophobic proposals represent a recurring trend in American history. From anti-Chinese immigrant laws in the late 1800s to the mass incarceration of Japanese immigrants (and Japanese Americans) during the mid-1900s to the mass deportation of Mexican immigrants (and their descendants) during the mid-1900s, Asian immigrants and Latina/o immigrants have historically been victimized by the state and its brutal agents. While it's too easy to just blame Trump and Republicans for xenophobic policies and programs, Democrats have also led these racist attacks against immigrants of color. Japanese immigrants (and Japanese Americans), for instance, were forced into internment camps by then-President Franklin Delano Roosevelt (FDR)—the iconic Democratic leader.

In his anti-immigration rhetoric and racist policies, without question, Trump wants to go back to the dark days of American history to "Make America White Again!"

TWENTY-THREE

City of Los Angeles Should Regulate Street Vendors

Joaquin Montes Huerta and Dr. Alvaro Huerta

We will never forget a disturbing incident that we witnessed several years ago in Boyle Heights while purchasing *pan dulce* at El Gallo Bakery. No, we didn't witness a Chicano teen engaging in graffiti or gang activity. Instead, we observed the police citing, handcuffing and confiscating the goods of an elderly Latino. Keeping a safe distance from the police to avoid being arrested for interfering in a so-called crime scene, we patiently waited for the man to be released to inquire about his alleged crime. While we originally assumed that he was selling contraband, we soon learned about the major "problem" impacting the mean streets of Los Angeles: the sale of sliced mangos, watermelon, *jicama*, cantaloupe, coconut and oranges. As a street vendor, he was also fully stocked with lime, salt and powdered *chile*. Shouldn't the Los Angeles Police Department (LAPD), with its finite resources, focus on real criminals, like politicians or government staff who take bribes from lobbyists and developers?

In 2015, as the Los Angeles City Council considers legalizing street vending, we're baffled about the city's draconian approach against Latina/o street vendors. Given the many problems that plague the nation's second-largest city, in lieu of targeting hard-working Latina/o petty-entrepreneurs, shouldn't the city focus on drug dealers, slum lords and unscrupulous employers who engage in wage-theft? Speaking of criminals, let's not forget about those who engage in white collar crimes who can afford lawyers to defend themselves and avoid jail.

It's no secret that city leaders cherish being a global city, whether they're competing for international investors, professional football teams

85

or global sports events. By showcasing City of Los Angeles to the world, for example, Mayor Eric Garcetti and City Council members invested significant time, money and energy to secure a bid for the 2024 Summer Olympics, with its inherent financial risks. Yet, when it comes to legalizing street vending, city leaders lack the same sense of urgency to provide street vendors with permits to work without fear of the law. More specifically, street vendors should operate without bureaucratic obstacles or obscene limits.

This is not a new problem for the City of Los Angeles. Food researchers have traced street vending in Los Angeles as far back as the 1870s. This includes *tamaleros*, or *tamale* sellers. In their recently published books, Gustavo Arellano and Farley Elliot provide us with excellent details and facts in documenting this fascinating history. This includes Arellano's *Taco USA: How Mexican Food Conquered America* and Elliot's *Los Angeles Street Food: A History from Tamaleros to Taco Trucks*. In these insightful books, we learn that the City of Los Angeles originally regulated Mexican *tamaleros* by the late 1800s and outright banned street vending on public streets by the early 1900s.

Today, despite being banned, Latina/o immigrant street vendors (and other racialized groups) continue to sell *tamales* and other products on the streets. By operating in the informal economy or unregulated economy, street vendors who sell food and other goods shouldn't be confused or lumped with real criminals. To better understand the nature of the informal economy, policymakers and the police should differentiate between "licit" and "illicit" economic activities on the streets. For example, while selling *tamales* or *pupusas* constitute "licit" activities, peddling marijuana or cocaine represent "illicit" actions.

In December of 2011, to provide relief to street vendors, a citywide coalition of organizations launched the Los Angeles Street Vendor Campaign to pressure the city to regulate this informal sector. Participating groups include the East Los Angeles Community Corporation (ELACC), Leadership for Urban Renewal Network (LURN), Coalition for Humane Immigrant Rights of Los Angeles (CHIRLA), Urban & Environmental Policy Institute (UEPI) at Occidental College, Public Counsel, Los Angeles Food Policy Council (LAFPC) and others. Participants also include public interest lawyers, scholars and pro-immigrant advocates. The street vendors themselves to an active and leadership role in this campaign. On a consistent basis, campaign leaders have been advocating for city leaders to legalize street vending, including implementing a citywide permit system, incentivizing healthy foods and providing support to the vendors.

In response, the City Council has prolonged a relatively straightforward process of decriminalizing street vending. City leaders continue to drag their feet by contemplating numerous permit options, such as citywide versus district-wide permit plans, and engaging in endless discussions about complex legislation and legal language.

Meanwhile, on July 29, 2015, to the dismay of street vendors and their advocates, the City Council voted 12–3 to ban street vending at public parks. From a public policy perspective, does it make sense for a Latina/o immigrant to pay a $250 fine and face a potential misdemeanor charge for selling a strawberry *paleta*?

Enough with this nonsense!

As documented in a 2015 report by the Economic Roundtable, *Sidewalk Stimulus: Economic and Geographic Impact of Los Angeles Street Vendors*, street vendors provide positive benefits to the city. "From food to merchandise," according to the researchers, "50,000 sidewalk entrepreneurs stimulate the local economy by generating $434 million in economic activity" (Liu, Burns and Flaming 20). This well-documented report also finds that this unregulated sector generates employment for Latina/o immigrants, complements brick-and-motor businesses, promotes public safety and encourages social interaction in the city. Similarly, UCLA summer students, in a 2015 class titled "Mapping L.A. Street Vendors: Economic and Cultural Practice in the Global City," shed light on this vulnerable immigrant labor niche, where the students interviewed resilient and hard-working street vendors.

In order to stop wasting time and getting down to business, Mayor Garcetti and the City Council should legalize street vending without burdensome restrictions and value the Latina/o immigrant street vendors' key characteristics: strong work ethic, family orientation and entrepreneurial spirit.

TWENTY-FOUR

Saturday Night Live Must Dump GOP Candidate Donald J. Trump

Dr. Alvaro Huerta

As the leading Republican presidential candidate, Donald J. Trump is neither a joke nor a clown. He must be taken seriously, as the potential GOP nominee, especially given the weak pool of Republican candidates. Apart from his racist rhetoric against Mexican immigrants, if elected, Trump plans to mass deport over 11 million undocumented immigrants and dreams to strip citizenship from the U.S.-born children of undocumented immigrants. Is this the moral imperative that drives his slogan, "Make America Great Again"? If so, what does that say about the deep-rooted racism found among a significant segment of the Republican base? Maybe he should be more honest and replace his slogan with: "Make America White Again"? Thus, when *Saturday Night Live* invites Trump to host the sketch-comedy show on November 7, 2015, it only legitimizes and normalizes Trump's racist tropes, xenophobic narratives and inhumane policies.

While many political pundits, opponents and comics have reduced Trump to a caricature, based on his outrageous and boisterous claims, his critics and those who poke fun of him underestimate the inhumane consequences of a Trump presidency. Throughout history, we have seen how members of the dominant society have classified and objectified racialized minorities and immigrants in order to exploit them for their labor power and land. For example, as part of their mission to steal the ancestral lands of the indigenous people of this land and relocate them to reservations, Americans leaders and average citizens (mostly white folks) conveniently labeled Native Americans as "heathens," "savages" and "criminals."

Moreover, when the U.S. government launched a genocide campaign against the indigenous people of this land, such as the Indian Removal Act of 1830, American leaders implemented this racist and inhumane policy without too much resistance from a white citizenry who directly benefited from what is tragically referred to as "The Trail of Tears."

In the case of Mexicans in *el norte*, during the twentieth century, the U.S. government launched mass deportation campaigns against non-citizens and citizens. For example, during the Great Depression, under the so-called "Mexican Repatriation," American leaders found a convenient scapegoat in brown people, during a time when white Americans were experiencing extremely high levels of unemployment. Similarly, in 1954, under "Operation Wetback," the U.S. government carried out another mass deportation campaign—focusing on cities, since agricultural workers were in high demand. Ironically, then-President Dwight "Ike" Eisenhower heralded "Operation Wetback" during a time when the U.S. was experiencing a post–WWII economic boom.

In a time when globalization is on the rise, we see American leaders, like Trump, who seek to repeat America's dark past. For instance, as Trump double-downs on his idiotic U.S.-Mexico wall, which Mexico will miraculously "pay for," he should learn from then-President Ronald Reagan's 1987 speech about Germany's Berlin Wall—a wall that divided West and East Germany, where the Soviet Union occupied the East. In this famous speech, held in West Germany, Reagan had a clear message for then-Soviet Union leader Mikhail Gorbachev: "Tear down this Wall!"

However, instead of following Reagan's example of tearing down walls that impede human progress and pose obstacles for trade with a friendly neighbor, Mexico, Trump likens his huge wall, with a "big beautiful door," to the Great Wall of China—a wall that was built over 2,200 years ago!

When will the verbal and physical abuse against the Mexican people in *el norte* stop? What did this large and important racialized group do to deserve such disdain and hatred from American leaders and millions of white citizens? Don't Mexican immigrants and Chicanas/os (Mexican Americans) also pay taxes? How about all of the deaths of Chicano soldiers in America's wars, from WWII to Korea, from Iraq to Afghanistan? Doesn't the ultimate sacrifice of Chicano blood in the battlefield count for anything?

Moreover, didn't workers of Mexican heritage help build this country with their labor power and determination, despite losing half of their territory in an imperialist U.S. war against Mexico from 1846 to 1848? Apart from their labor contributions, what about the many contributions that promote diversity and enrich this country in the areas of the physical environment, architecture, environmentalism, informality, law, history, civil rights, art, dance, theater, comedy, film, music, literature, sports, language, food, drink and much more? And, let's not forget their/our strong work ethic, entrepreneurial spirit and family-oriented values.

As long as popular television programs, like *Saturday Night Live*, provide Trump with a platform to legitimize his racist views and inhumane policies against Mexican immigrants, powerful players, such as *SNL* executive producer Lorne Michaels and NBC Universal's CEO Stephen B. Burke, only reinforce the rampant racial attacks and catastrophic public policies against *los de abajo*/those on the bottom.

TWENTY-FIVE

U.S. Courts Maintain Undocumented Immigrants in the Shadows

Dr. Alvaro Huerta

As millions of Americans prepare for Thanksgiving celebrations with their families and friends, eating turkey and watching football, undocumented immigrants remain in the shadows. Recently, the Fifth U.S. Circuit Court of Appeals upheld a court injunction against President Barack Obama's 2014 immigration executive orders. In his executive orders, Obama sought to temporarily shield an estimated 5 million undocumented immigrants from deportation. This includes the Deferred Action for Parents of Americans (DAPA) program and an expansion of the 2012 Deferred Action for Childhood Arrivals (DACA) program.

Not long after Obama's 2014 immigration executive orders, twenty-six Republican governors wasted no time in finding a conservative friend in U.S. District Judge Andrew S. Hanen from Brownsville, Texas, who quickly ordered his court injunction. By appealing this injunction, the Obama administration experienced another defeat, by a 2-to-1 ruling, from the conservative-majority Fight Circuit. Consequently, on November 20, 2015, the Obama administration petitioned the Supreme Court to review and reverse this recent ruling. Ideally, should the Obama administration prevail, it aims to implement these executive orders before Obama leaves the White House.

While the Republican governors against DAPA and DACA argued that Obama's immigration executive orders disregarded administrative review procedures, created financial burdens for states, such as costs for driver licenses, and superseded Congress in re-creating new immigration laws, among other legal issues, it's crystal clear to me that both programs only provide temporary and limited relief from deportation for 5 million undocumented immigrants.

Unlike then-President Ronald Reagan's 1986 Immigration Reform and Control Act (IRCA), which provided over 3 million undocumented immigrants with citizenship, neither DAPA nor DACA provides a pathway to citizenship to those who live and work in America's shadows. Should the Supreme Court grant review of the case, Dean Kevin R. Johnson (UC Davis Law School) and Dean Erwin Chemerinsky (UC Irvine School of Law) argue that there's a real chance for Obama to prevail. While recognizing the unpredictable nature of the Supreme Court on rulings, both distinguished legal scholars refer to *Arizona v. United States* (2012), where the Supreme Court ruled against Arizona's controversial immigration law, SB 1070. Should the Supreme Court review and rule in favor of the Obama administration, led by Solicitor Gen. Donald Verrilli Jr., millions of undocumented immigrants will finally receive temporary relief from deportation.

Republican leaders, in catering to mostly white voters and extremists, have prioritized xenophobia as a key political platform. By doing so, they blame America's woes on Latina/o immigrants. This obviously doesn't sit well with the majority of Latina/o voters. Thus, when it comes to future elections, Latinas/os won't forget those who vilified and scapegoated their family members, friends, acquaintances, co-workers and neighbors. Similarly, given that immigration represents an important issue for Asian and Pacific Islanders, they, too, won't forget those who disrespected and offended members of their communities—with or without legal status.

When it comes to future elections, Republican leaders don't appear interested in securing the Latina/o vote, in addition to the Asian and Pacific Islander vote. From filing lawsuits against Obama's immigration executive orders to refusing to pass comprehensive immigration reform to deporting millions of undocumented immigrants to proposing to revoke citizenship from their U.S.-born children of undocumented immigrants, Republicans should learn from their failed 2012 presidential nominee, former Gov. Mitt Romney, with his "ingenious" immigration plan: self-deportation.

While Republicans may secure electoral victories in the short-term, given the dramatic demographic changes taking place in this country, where we're witnessing the browning of America, the GOP will surely experience failure in the long-term.

TWENTY-SIX

The Shameful Case of Latino Republican Leaders

Sen. Ted Cruz and Sen. Marco Rubio

Dr. Alvaro Huerta

Growing up on the mean streets of East Los Angeles, I, like many of my childhood friends, feared the police more than the neighborhood gang, Big Hazard. Specifically, we dreaded Latino cops, since they had a reputation of being more brutal than their white peers toward us—poor Chicano kids from the projects. By verbally and physically harassing us, the Latino cops reinforced their loyalty to their white peers in particular and police department in general. Similarly, in the Republican presidential nomination contest, we can clearly see how the two Latino candidates, Sen. Marco Rubio (R-FL) and Sen. Ted Cruz (R-TX), go the extra mile to demonstrate their loyalty to their white peers and xenophobic political party, the GOP.

Hence, instead of glowing in an important historical moment, where two so-called Latino leaders represent viable candidates for the highest office in the United States, Rubio and Cruz have engaged in a vitriol debate over their mutual disdain of Latina/o undocumented immigrants. The ongoing duel between the senators focuses on who supports amnesty or a pathway to citizenship for undocumented immigrants, as if it's a "sin" or bad thing to do so, representing a low point for both candidates. Speaking of low points, during the last Republican debate, the senators tussled over the Spanish language. When Cruz questioned Rubio's conservative credentials for supporting President Barack Obama's immigration executive orders in Spanish on Univision, Rubio, as usual, refused to acknowledge any sympathies for those who live and work in America's shadows.

Apart from demonstrating their anti-Latina/o immigrant credentials, it's difficult to differentiate the Latino Republican candidates with the bombastic Donald J. Trump and his racist positions on immigration. From supporting the mass deportation of Mexican immigrants—like in the inhumane case of "Operation Wetback" of the mid-1950s—to the construction of a huge wall—that Mexico will "miraculously" pay for—to the ban Muslims to this country, the Latino Republicans aim to emulate Trump. While Gov. John Kasich (R-OH) and former Gov. Jeb Bush (R-FL) have expressed their discontent with Trump's racist policy proposals against immigrants, the only Latino candidates in the GOP don't seem perturbed at all.

¡Qué lástima!

Given their anti-Latina/o immigrant agendas and lack of sympathy for the plight of immigrants, if either Rubio or Cruz manages to become the Republican nominee, how will the winner regain the trust and confidence of Latinas/os, as the largest racialized group in this country? Given that Latinas/os represent over 55 million citizens/residents in the U.S., as a key voting bloc, Latinas/os will remember both their friends and foes in future elections. Numerous surveys by Latino Decisions—as the leading Latina/o political opinion group—reveal that Latinas/os favor immigration as an important election issue.

Since Latinas/os and Asian Americans voted by a 3-to-1 margin to help elect (and re-elect) Barack Obama as President of the United States, Democrats will continue to hold a monopoly on these two voting blocs, especially given the anti-immigrant platform of the GOP. And let's not forget that many white Republicans, at a national level, won't embrace a Latino or Latina to lead this racist party. This cold reality makes it impossible for either Rubio or Cruz, as Latino Republicans—whether they like to be labeled this way or not—to ever prevail in a presidential election.

In the words of the Hollywood action hero and former Republican Governor of California, Arnold Schwarzenegger, I have four words— three of them in Spanish—for these pitiful Latino Republicans: *¡Hasta la vista*, baby!

TWENTY-SEVEN

Republican Policies and Christian Values

Inherent Contradictions?

Dr. Alvaro Huerta

As former Catholic and current atheist, I applaud Pope Francis' recent rebuke of Donald J. Trump and his wall fetish. Responding to a reporter about his views on Trump, on February 18, 2016, following his visit to the border city of Juárez, Mexico, Pope Francis famously said, "A person who thinks only about building walls, wherever they may be, and not building bridges, is not Christian. This is not the gospel" (Burke, CNN). While the bombastic xenophobe and main Republican presidential candidate wasted no time to defend his alleged Christian faith—Presbyterianism—he chastised Pope Francis and absurdly accused him of being a pawn of the Mexican government. Trump is talking about the same Mexican government leaders who hectored Pope Francis, while in Mexico City, for saying that the government fostered a society plagued with violence and drugs.

This didn't stop the "devout" Catholic and former presidential Republican candidate Jeb Bush, also known as "Low-energy Jeb" by Trump, to defend Trump. Given the anti-immigrant positions that Republican candidates have adopted to appeal to white voters, it seems to me that Pope Francis' public scolding of Trump also applies to the other Republican leaders. Hence, to better understand whether the GOP's extremist actions and mean-spirited rhetoric conflict with Christian values, let's explore a few popular Christian tenets and commandments. To avoid a theological debate, I'll just paraphrase a few, while providing some commentary.

"Thou shalt love thy neighbor . . .": This is a popular Christian tenet that many of us are familiar with since childhood. The last time I checked Google Earth, Mexico is our southern neighbor. Given that Mexico represents a friendly neighbor in diplomatic relations, trade agreements and tourism, why do Republican leaders continually bash our neighbor like a piñata at a kid's birthday party? While Latina/o immigrants may not live in the same neighborhoods as privileged Republican leaders, many of them do live in nearby neighborhoods and cities, making them neighbors. As neighbors, Latina/o immigrants represent a vital labor pool, particularly in the low-wage service sector, where privileged Republican leaders and millions of Americans benefit from their labor power and rendered services. This includes important services that Latina/o immigrants provide in this country, like childcare, elderly care, house cleaning, dry cleaning, landscape gardening, day laboring and much more. Latina/o immigrants also own and operate businesses that all Americans benefit from, like restaurants, auto repair shops, beauty salons, construction companies, legal firms, etc.

Doesn't the Republican leadership lack of love or respect for our neighbors—outside and inside of our borders—represent a violation of Christian values? It makes no sense to me. Yet, what do I know, I'm an atheist.

"Thou shalt not steal": While Republican leaders have no problem bashing Mexico and, especially, Mexicans for migrating to *el norte*, let's not forget that in 1848 the U.S. stole approximately half of Mexico's territory in the bloody spirit of Manifest Destiny. Does the fact that this land theft occurred over 150 years ago make it inconsequential in contemporary times? What about the legitimacy of the Treaty of Guadalupe Hidalgo of 1848 that ended the U.S. imperialist war against Mexico? Didn't it guarantee basic rights for the Mexicans who resided in the conquered territory? Speaking of treaties, how can the Mexican government hold the U.S. responsible for how Mexicans are mistreated in *el norte*? While I'm not a legal scholar on treaties, I'll consult with some Native American friends and colleagues for their expert opinion on treaty-related issues.

What about the labor power and wages the U.S. stole from blacks during slavery? The same labor, like immigrant labor, that helped make the U.S. the most powerful nation in the world. While the award-winning writer Ta-Nehisi Coates makes a compelling case for reparations for blacks or African Americans in his brilliant article, "The Case for Reparations," many American leaders reject this proposal. This includes President Barack Obama, as the first African American president. Regardless of the merits of this proposal, no one can ignore the fact that the U.S. benefited tremendously from slave labor.

"Thou shalt not murder": This represents another popular Christian commandment. Thus, for American leaders—both Republicans and Democrats—who supported the imperialist invasion of Iraq, causing mass murder, destruction and havoc, how can they, especially as so-called Christians, reconcile war with this commandment? While Trump correctly argues that the U.S. invaded Iraq under false pretenses (e.g., no weapons of mass destruction), he has taken a strong position in favor of killing suspected ISIS terrorists and their families. I assume that includes children?

Trump isn't the only one willing to kill innocent civilians in the war against ISIS. Sen. Ted Cruz (R-TX), desperately seeking to be "tougher" than Trump, wants to carpet bomb ISIS. What about all of the civilians who live nearby or the held hostage by ISIS? Ben Carson, as a "devout" Christian and presidential Republican candidate, is also willing to kill innocent civilians, including children, as part of this proposal. Let's not forget the always evasive Sen. Marco Rubio (R-FL), who doesn't seem bothered by the killings of innocent civilians in the war against ISIS. Is this a just or humane manner for Christians to wage war?

While preparing for my First Communion and attending mass at East Los Angeles' Santa Teresita Church many years ago, I can still recall a sermon from a priest about how it's easier for a camel to enter the eye of a needle than for a rich person to enter "heaven." I'll never forget this important lesson from my youth. So, my question is, once Trump dies, what's going to happen to him, as a so-called Christian, with his vast fortune (and debts?), luxury hotels, golf courses and the huge wall that he constantly fantasizes about?

TWENTY-EIGHT

An Open Letter to Clinton on Candidate Trouncing Trump in the General Election

Dr. Alvaro Huerta

Date: April 5, 2016
Dear Former Secretary of State Hilary Clinton:

On March 5, 2014, during my interview with Tavis Smiley, I predicted that you would become the 45th President of the United States. This doesn't mean, however, that I endorse your campaign, primarily due to your neo-liberal political agenda, deep Wall Street ties and hawkish foreign policy positions. In your book review of *World Order* by former Secretary of State Henry Kissinger (*The Washington Post*, September 4, 2014), for example, you expressed fondness for Kissinger—a war criminal. This probably explains your disastrous handling of the 2009 Honduran coup d'état, where the democratically elected president, José Manuel Zelaya, was overthrown by the military. If you believe in democracy in Latin America, why didn't you, as Secretary of State, cut diplomatic and military ties with Honduras' post-coup government?

Since you'll most likely face reality-television star Donald J. Trump in the general election—unless the GOP "fires" him during the Republican National Convention—I suggest that you take my advice to ensure victory against Trump—the more dangerous candidate.

Learn from the mistakes of the defeated GOP candidates. Given that the defeated GOP candidates, such as former-Gov. Jeb Bush, Gov. Chris Christy, Sen. Marco Rubio and Ben Carson, were mostly cordial toward Trump and failed miserably in debates with him, you should be relentless against this "orange" bully. While Trump appears to be a wounded candidate due to controversies related to his unconscionable treatment of women, he's still a formidable candidate.

Apart from unleashing a relentless attack against Trump, be cognizant of his childish name-calling tactics. Some of his victims include "Low-energy Jeb Bush," "Little Marco" and "Lying Ted Cruz." In the case of women, as you're aware, he's had really nasty things to say. Unfortunately, negative labels often work in politics and elsewhere when they're constantly repeated and when some people perceived them to be true or when there's some truth to them.

Since Trump doesn't play fair, don't play fair or by his rules. Just ask "Little Marco." Also, don't try to make sense of his confusing rhetoric or lack of logic. He probably doesn't believe many of the things that he says, since he often says outrageous things or outright lies to rattle his opponents.

Develop an effective campaign slogan. Part of Trump's popular appeal with a significant segment of the American population, especially the white working-class, centers on his ability to simplify his message. This starts with "his" effective campaign slogan: "Make America Great Again!" While effective from a marketing strategy, this slogan represents major problems for Latinas/os, African Americans, Asians and Native Americans due to America's racist past (and present). Yet, politically speaking, it serves its purpose. But Trump shouldn't get too much credit, since he copied this slogan from past campaigns. For instance, during Ronald Reagan's 1980 presidential campaign, Reagan used the "Make America Great Again" slogan in political buttons and posters. Trump isn't the only presidential candidate to copy a slogan from the past, however. In 2008, then-presidential candidate Barack Obama copied his effective "Yes We Can" slogan from the United Farm Workers' "*Sí, Se Puede.*" Unlike Trump, when asked, Obama does give the UFW credit. More specifically, it was Dolores Huerta, as co-founder of the UFW with Cesar Chavez, who coined this term.

Being a more experienced and knowledgeable candidate on public policy issues and foreign affairs isn't enough. You must also be able to connect and communicate succinctly with common people with a hopeful and inspirational message.

Counter Trump's message to America's Angry White People (AWP) problem. Trump is very effective when catering to white people who have anger issues. To appeal to this core group, Trump launched his presidential campaign with his infamous attacks against Mexican immigrants, referring to them as "drug dealers," "criminals" and "rapists." Trump is no dummy. He's playing on the fears of white working-class individuals/families and some of their hardships: wage-stagnation, unemployment, outsourcing of jobs, lack of access to health insurance, rise in drug addiction and high premature deaths. Oh, I almost forgot: many Angry White

People (AWP) also have a pet peeve with a major demographic change taking place: the browning of America.

To counter Trump's pseudo-populist message, you must embrace Sen. Bernie Sanders' political platform to explain why so many working-class and middle-class individuals/families are suffering under American capitalism. Moreover, while you must take a pay-cut from your "huuuge" Wall Street speaking fees, you must also do what's morally right for the vast majority of people in this country. By the way, don't forget to incorporate institutional racism in your political platform. This is something that Sanders ignores or forgets to do, which explains his mostly white audiences at political rallies.

Don't pander to Latinas/os. As illustrated by the "Viva Kennedy" electoral outreach campaign (1959 to 1963) by Mexican Americans to support John F. Kennedy against Richard Nixon in the 1960 presidential election, Latinas/os have been a loyal voting bloc to the Democratic Party. This includes Barack Obama's presidential election of 2008 and re-election of 2012, where Latinas/os, supporting Obama by an estimated 75 percent, played a pivotal role in these campaigns. So what have Latinas/os received in return for their loyalty? Well, let's start with residential segregation, poor public schools, lack of access to higher education, rampant cases of police abuse, high rates of youth unemployment and unacceptable rates incarceration. And, speaking of President Obama or the "Deporter-in-Chief," let's not forget that Obama deported over 2.5 million undocumented immigrants during his time in office.

It's not enough to speak Spanish during elections or eat at a Mexican restaurant with a mariachi group playing in the background or have famous brown actors speak on your behalf to address the needs of Latinas/os. Similarly, it's not enough to denounce Obama's inhumane deportation record or Trump's xenophobic rhetoric. To be an advocate and a true friend of Latinas/os, it's more about transforming the same racist institutions and inhumane programs/policies that perpetuate a profit-driven and immoral system at the expense of *los de abajo*/those on the bottom.

TWENTY-NINE

Urban Planners of the World Unite Against Trump

Dr. Alvaro Huerta

As an urban planning scholar and a son of Mexican immigrants, I implore all urban planning scholars, practitioners and students to stand up against Donald J. Trump—the Republican nominee for President of the United States. I'm aware that some planning scholars and practitioners will argue that we shouldn't become partisan, taking sides in an election where the American people will elect the next leader of the most powerful nation in the world. However, given that I'm an independent, I counter that there comes a time in history when we must unite as urban planners—as experts on how communities, cities and regions function—and citizens/residents of this country to take a moral stance. We must voice our collective opposition against a racist Republican leader who embraced the prospect of a housing crises, proposed a deportation force to deport over 11 million undocumented immigrants and called for a ban on all Muslim immigrants.

These three examples, just to name a few, directly relate to the diligent and professional work of urban planners in public and private spheres. First, urban planners have historically focused on housing issues, especially for the most vulnerable among us. For instance, after Jacob Riis published his class book, *How the Other Half Lives: Studies among the Tenements of New York* (1890), shedding light on the deplorable working and living conditions of European immigrants and the poor in overcrowded cities, it didn't take long for government officials and future urban planners to seek housing solutions, such as housing codes that we currently take for granted.

For Trump, as a real estate mogul with several corporate bankrupt-cies, a housing crisis that negatively impacts millions of Americans and immigrants, represents a business opportunity to "go in and buy like crazy." Should Trump prevail against former Secretary of State Hillary Clinton on November 8, 2016, we can forget about government interven-ing to assist working-class families, racialized minorities and immigrants to secure safe and affordable housing. For someone like Trump, when it comes to housing and properties, it's more about generating profits and supporting wealthy investors based on depreciated real estate values. For instance, will the Housing and Urban Development (HUD) become an agent or a broker to facilitate business interests for The Trump Organiza-tion and Trump's business partners?

Secondly, as for Trump's deportation force that will arrest, detain and deport over 11 million undocumented immigrants, will urban planners—along with architects, engineers, construction contractors, etc.—be re-cruited to design, build and implement the infrastructure for this propo-sal? More specifically, given that the Department of Homeland Security (DHS) and the private sector don't have enough detention centers to house an additional 11 million undocumented immigrants, will urban planners, etc., become complicit in this cruel megaproject? Or, will Presi-dent Trump use eminent domain—a powerful planning tool, where the government claims or confiscates private property "for the public good"—to take possession of all football stadiums, baseball fields, soccer fields and basketball arenas—in addition to building new ones—to de-tain millions of undocumented immigrants? Speaking of eminent do-main, let's not forget that it was used by the City of Los Angeles during the mid-1900s to displace/remove the Chicana/o community of Chavez Ravine to make room for Dodger Stadium and the Los Angeles Dodgers.

Thirdly, Trump's immigration proposal to ban an entire group of peo-ple (i.e., Muslims), compromising of about 1.6 billion individuals world-wide, goes against the professional ethics of urban planners, as stipulated by the American Institute of Certified Planners (AICP): "We shall seek social justice by working to expand choice and opportunity for all per-sons, recognizing a special responsibility to plan for the needs of the disadvantaged and to promote racial and economic integration. We shall urge the alteration of policies, institutions, and decisions that oppose such needs."

As a result, when a Republican leader like Trump targets all Muslims or makes gross generalizations about Mexican immigrants, referring to them/us as "drug dealers," "criminals" and "rapists," urban planners and planning organizations—e.g., academic, professional, student—must ve-hemently oppose these xenophobic propositions. Given that historians and others (e.g., "Writers on Trump") have also organized themselves against Trump, many more professional and working-class groups, etc., should do likewise.

Given the recent violent attacks in Orlando (U.S.), Paris (France), Istanbul (Turkey) and elsewhere against innocent people—where we've all become vulnerable to terrorist acts—we must fight back against hate-driven proposals and racist rhetoric by American leaders, as epitomized by Trump. Trump's racist and fascist rhetoric, along with the GOP's anti-immigrant platform, only serves to incite more violence—domestically and internationally.

Instead of peddling racial division and "ugly" walls, like Trump's daily rants and tweets, as the world has become more interconnected through commerce, technology, social media and immigration, we, as urban planners and architects, must all work to build racial unity and "beautiful" bridges.

THIRTY

The Hustler

Trump and the Mean Streets of East Los Angeles

Dr. Alvaro Huerta

On the first day of class, I always inform my university students that I hold "three" doctorates. This includes: (1) earning a PhD from UC Berkeley; (2) spending over a decade as a highly effective community organizer; and (3) surviving one of the toughest neighborhoods in the country — East Los Angeles' Ramona Gardens housing project (or Big Hazard projects). While I've relied on my research skills and organizing background to criticize Donald J. Trump, as the Republican presidential nominee, I've also depended on my street smarts to deconstruct his extremist politics, bold lies and erratic behavior. While political foes, pundits, cable news anchors and journalists are bewildered by Trump, I grew up with his type: wannabe tough guy, bully and hustler. To deal with Trump, we must view him through these typologies, among others, such as xenophobe, racist, money-grubber, misogynist and pathological liar.

If I had the opportunity to debate Trump, I would paraphrase then-Sen. Lloyd Bentsen (D-TX) when he demolished then-Sen. Dan Quayle (R-IN) in the 1988 vice-presidential debate: "Trump, I grew up with tough guys. I knew tough guys. Tough guys were friends of mine. Trump, you're no tough guy."

It's amazing to me that Trump gets away with a "tough guy" persona, boasting about punching protestors in the face, killing families of suspected terrorists, waterboarding suspected terrorists and being cavalier about the use of guns and bombs (including nukes!) to resolve domestic and international conflicts. This is the same so-called tough guy who secured five deferments to avoid the Vietnam War, according to Steve Eder and Dave Phillips of the *New York Times* (August 1, 2016).

In his seventy years of life, has Trump ever experienced a situation involving guns or violence? Growing up in the projects, I witnessed and experienced many deadly and dangerous situations. As a teenager, I witnessed the fatal shooting of a young Chicano at a backyard party. Also, as a sixteen-year-old, while teaching myself how to drive, I luckily evaded a dangerous situation when a cop pointed his gun at me. My so-called alleged crime consisted of failing to make a complete stop!

To prove his toughness, Trump should visit my old barrio—without private bodyguards, Secret Service agents, the police or *la migra* for protection. Once there, let's see him restate his racist claims that Mexican immigrants are "drug dealers," "criminals" and "rapists." If he can't repeat these racist generalizations directly to the people he's insulting, he's a coward. On a related point, during his recent trip to Mexico, why didn't "super macho" Trump directly demand that Mexican President Enrique Peña Nieto pay for his stupid wall?

Since he's not a real tough guy, by picking on one of the most vulnerable groups in this country, Trump has cemented his bully credentials. Like the bullies roaming our schools, neighborhoods, parks and congressional offices, Trump preys on individuals who can't defend themselves. He behaves like a sixth grader bully who insults third graders and takes their lunch money. By supporting Trump, millions of Americans, especially white folks, only legitimize his brutish, infantile and racist behavior—domestically and internationally—whereby perpetuating or reinforcing the "Ugly American" reputation.

Moreover, Trump is a hustler. While the term "hustle" or "to hustle" has positive and negative connotations on the streets, as it pertains to Trump and his ilk, it refers to individuals who take advantage of others for personal gains. We had a few of them in the projects. For example, after lending $20 to a childhood "friend," he hustled me by not paying me back—which, I later learned, he never intended to do so. I also later learned that he had stiffed other friends. On one memorable occasion, a street hustler sold my sister a car battery that he originally stole from her red Nissan 208Z the prior night. (Fortunately, he gave her a discount.) Eventually, these individuals secure bad reputations as hustlers, where they can't be trusted, like Trump.

In terms of his business reputation, in addition to lawsuits surrounding Trump University, Trump has been involved in many legal cases by many individuals and vendors who didn't receive payment for their services. According to media reports, Trump's companies have been involved in thousands of lawsuits during the past thirty years, where, on many cases, he or his companies have been accused of not paying bills for services rendered, etc.

Furthermore, hustlers will say anything you want to hear to satisfy their self-interests. They conveniently change their message or tone when it benefits them. Just ask the former members of Trump's National Hispanic Advisory Council, like Alfonso Aguilar and Jacob Monty. Both of these Latino Republicans resigned from this council after listening to Trump's extremist, anti-immigration speech in Arizona on August 31, 2016. I'm astonished that it took so long for these idiotic Latino Republicans to learn that Trump was hustling them and the American public. Basically, like the black Republican supporters and immoral surrogates in Trump's corner (e.g., Ben Carson, Omarosa Manigault), these small-minded Latinos were used as token brown faces in the mostly white Republican presidential campaign and Republican Party.

Finally, given that Trump always boasts about being a winner, there's no doubt in my expert opinion that he'll always win in one category: America's biggest hustler.

THIRTY-ONE

An Open Letter to President Donald J. Trump

Confessions of an "Anchor Baby"

Dr. Alvaro Huerta

Date: January 20, 2017
Dear President J. Donald Trump:

Now that you've become the 45th President of the United States, I have a confession: I'm a so-called "anchor baby." Given that you represent the "great white hope" to "Make America Great Again!," I'm confessing in exchange to be pardoned for my "crime." Honestly, I didn't know that being born to Mexican immigrants on work visas violated the law or that pesky little thing called the Fourteenth Amendment of the Constitution. If I would've known of your novel interpretation of our Constitution, since you're the guardian of the "white American Dream," I would've pleaded to doctors in my mother's womb to be aborted. Oh, I forgot, Republicans don't believe in abortion. Does the GOP make exceptions for brown fetuses?

By the way, I'm also asking for my late Mexican parents to be pardoned posthumously for their so-called "sins." Before you do so, however, I want to remind you that they weren't "criminals," "rapists" and "drug dealers." To find the truth about my parent's so-called shady past, especially since I know how much you value "facts" or discovering the truth, like your "investigators" in Hawaii—the ones looking for then-President Barack Obama's "real birth certificate"—to look into my parent's past activities for the sake of national security.

While then-President Obama "wasted" his time with ISIS, fortunately, you've enlightened us about the apocalyptic threats that Latina/o immigrants pose to the U.S. In fact, my mother, as a domestic worker for over forty years, must have stolen tons of Charmin toilet paper (one-ply) from the white families she "deceitfully" served. Also, since my father worked as farmworker during the Bracero Program of the mid-twentieth century, he "surely" moonlighted as a drug dealer. As a *bracero*, my father "must have" worked for Joaquín "El Chapo" Guzmán—the Mexican drug lord who escaped from a Mexican prison. It doesn't matter that El Chapo was in his teens during the early 1960s. Who cares about these type of facts or small details? I'm "so happy" that we have "alternative facts" or "fake news."

Speaking of El Chapo, I congratulate you on showing him who's the real *jefe* via Twitter. Only someone like yourself, a graduate of The Wharton School of Business, can outsmart and instill fear in a Mexican drug lord. I bet Sen. John McCain (R-AZ), the so-called POW "traitor," couldn't handle El Chapo, *mano a mano*, like you. Once you personally pursue El Chapo, I suggest that you select Duane "Dog" Chapman or "Dog the Bounty Hunter" as Secretary of State to help you track him down in Mexico. While you're at it, make sure to ask the Mexican government for enough *pesos* to build your fantasy wall!

Once you build your gold-plated Trump Wall—surrounded with casinos, golf courses and infinity pools—it will put the Great Wall of China to shame. Heck, if Mexico fails to deliver the billions of *pesos* for your stupid wall, you can simply negotiate with the Chinese for a portion of their wall in exchange for the oil money you'll "secure" from re-invading Iraq. It's amazing how easy international diplomacy has become, now that you've become the leader of the free-market world.

As part of your "dream" to "Make America White Again!," especially by ridding the country of all those "pesky" brown people, you should relocate the White House to the "beacon" of "American exceptionalism": the Mar-a-Lago Club in Palm Beach, Florida.

THIRTY-TWO

The Hustler 2.0

President Trump

Dr. Alvaro Huerta

On several occasions, I've argued that Donald J. Trump was hustling the American public. Now, "thanks" to the help of the then-FBI Director James Comey for publicly discussing the frivolous email case against Hillary Clinton, the election interference from the Russian state and meddling by WikiLeaks' Julian Assange, Trump—as President of the United States—has continued to hustle the American public. Given his mastery to hustle people over his lifetime, "his" next book should be titled "The Art of the American Hustle."

In a nutshell, a hustler represents an individual who will say and do anything—without remorse or guilt—to serve his or her self-interest. While critics have labeled Trump many applicable terms, such as racist, erratic, narcissistic, serial liar and thin-skinned, etc., I find that that the term "hustler" effectively describes his twisted rhetoric and immoral actions.

When they speak or act, hustlers can't be believed or trusted. I should know, since I grew up on the mean streets of East Los Angeles, where I encountered many of them. Also, as an established scholar, public policy analyst and former community organizer, I've studied and observed hustlers at the local, state and national level. This includes politicians (Republicans and Democrats), government officials, private developers, the police and other powerful individuals who hustle the American public to serve their self-interests.

Apart from Trump, Congressman Paul D. Ryan (R-Wis.) is an excellent example of a hustler. While Ryan portrays himself as a so-called "sensible" policy "wonk" who "cares" about the American people, his sinister obsession to repeal and replace the Affordable Care Act (ACA) or Obamacare represents an atrocious and inhumane political agenda. As House Speaker, Ryan led the GOP's successful efforts to rush a so-called health plan that will wreak havoc on millions of Americans.

While Ryan's previously failed "health plan" would've left 24 million Americans without healthcare, according to the Congressional Budget Office (CBO), the negative impacts of his recently passed so-called health plan, named the American Health Care Act (AHCA), appears to have similar catastrophic results for millions of Americans. If this is such a "great plan," as Trump claims, why not allow for the CBO to conduct a thorough analysis and provide a score?

Speaking of the "orange" elephant in the room, as the "Hustler 2.0," Trump has argued that pre-existing conditions will be covered in the GOP's efforts to repeal and replace Obamacare. However, according to many analysts and reporters, such as Michael Hiltzik of the *Los Angeles Times* (May 4, 2017) who writes that AHCA "allows states to opt out of ACA rules prohibiting insurers from charging sick people higher premiums." This is like the GOP passing a law that allows states to opt out of federal minimum wage standards, child labor protections and anti-racist measures in public and private spheres (e.g., no "whites only" lunch counters in the South). That is, according to the GOP, the federal government shouldn't interfere if states want to deprive their residents from basic services and protections, like healthcare, that all people deserve as a right, not a privilege.

Also, let's not forget about Trumps stupid border wall. Originally, Trump told us, over and over, that Mexico was going to pay for it. Now, as the leader of the most powerful nation in the world, he wants American taxpayers to pay for it, where Mexico will magically reimburse us in the future.

In terms of NAFTA (North American Free Trade Agreement), Trump originally called it "the worst trade deal in the history of this country" in a speech in Pennsylvania (June 28, 2016), vowing to reverse it. Now, after a couple of phone calls with the leaders of Mexico and Canada, Trump will re-negotiate NAFTA with his "friendly" trading partners. If that's not a "huuuge" hustle, I don't know what is?

I can go on and on about China, Russia, NATO and North Korea, but what's the point?

Trying to keep up with the "Hustler 2.0" will only make "your head spin," as Trump famously says when he's boasting about something that he's clearly clueless about! Actually, apart from being a hustler, there's a term that Mexicans—on both sides of *la frontera*—use for shameless individuals (or those who lack shame) which aptly describes Trump: *sinvergüenza*.

Speaking of *sinvergüenza*, this pejorative term also applies to Ryan and all Republicans who publicly rejoiced about attacking healthcare and undermining other public services for the benefit of millions of Americans.

MEXICANS IN EL NORTE WILL
SURVIVE THE "HUSTLER-IN CHIEF"

I recently returned from a "Monthly Mexican Meeting" (MMM) in Los Angeles, California. At these "secret" meetings, all individuals of Mexican origin gather at 3:00 a.m. in towns, cities, counties and regions throughout the country, while the hustler Donald J. Trump is too busy on Twitter. This includes millions of individuals, minus the self-loathing Mexicans who voted for Trump. In 2016, according to U.S. Census data, there were approximately 36.3 million individuals of Mexican origin in the U.S., representing the largest Latina/o sub-group. While I was born in Sacramento, California, spending most of my life in this country, I spent the first four years of my life in Tijuana (Baja California, Mexico). Thus, I have solid Mexican credentials to lead the Los Angeles-based meetings.

Where exactly do we meet and how come we haven't been discovered? Well, we gather inside of taco trucks, hotels, college campuses, restaurants, churches, baseball stadiums and many other places, where many Mexicans and Mexican Americans toil long hours while many white Americans get their beauty sleep. While our main agenda item consists of the "The Taco-Truck-in-Every-Corner Campaign," we also discuss our traits and virtues that guide our daily lives: to be resilient, proud and generous, etc. Since the military conquest of Mexico by the Americans in 1848, for instance, Mexicans in *el norte* continue to survive and, for some, thrive.

As a resilient people, what can Trump do to us that we haven't already experienced during the past 500 years, dating back to the days of the bloody and greedy Spanish *conquistadores* (1519–1521)? In response to his racist rhetoric against Mexican immigrants, Mexicans wasted no time in composing anti-Trump *corridos* and creating Trump piñatas. At any given birthday party in *el norte*, for a Mexican kid to hit a Trump piñata with a broom or baseball bat represents what President Barack Obama refers to as a "teachable moment."

In addition to being resilient, Mexicans are a proud people. If you don't believe me, just attend a U.S.-Mexico soccer game in Pasadena, California, to see how many fans wear jerseys of *El Tricolor* at the Rose Bowl? Like millions of Mexicans, I screamed at the top of my lungs after viewing (on television) Mexico's 2–1 glorious victory against the U.S. in

Columbus, Ohio (on November 11, 2016). For many Mexicans, it makes no difference if Americans possess more financial capital or human capital (e.g., education). Mexican pride or happiness isn't contingent on accumulated capital or earned university degrees. This doesn't imply that they/we don't aspire to earn more money or pursue higher education. However, what does it matter if you're extremely rich or highly educated, but you suffer from poor ethics or low morals, like Trump?

Moreover, at our last meeting, we also celebrated our generosity. While we continue to be scapegoated for America's ills, we give more to this country than we receive. This is especially the case for undocumented immigrants or those without legal status. Millions of undocumented Mexican immigrants pay into the system with their labor power and taxes, yet don't qualify for key federal benefits, such as Social Security and Medicare. We can "thank" then-President Bill Clinton for his Welfare Reform Act of 1996 or the Personal Responsibility and Work Opportunity Reconciliation Act of 1996, which denied undocumented immigrant from receiving federal benefits and services.

Also, throughout my life, I've found Mexicans to be very generous and hospitable. To verify my claim, I encourage any American citizen (non-Latinas/os in particular) to visit a random home (with permission, of course) in a poor or working-class Mexican neighborhood (on either side of the border). By doing so, without being asked, he or she will be served food and drink by the Mexican hosts—even if it's the last piece of chicken they have to consume!

In fact, Mexicans are so generous that once the *gringos* started to settle in Mexico (what is now Texas) during the early 1800s, when my ancestors said *"Mi casa es su casa,"* as I've previously stated, the Americans took them literally and took their/our *casa*! Approximately 200 years later, despite being "foreigners in our own land," we're still here and not going anywhere.

THIRTY-THREE

An Open Letter to Gov. Jerry Brown on California Becoming a Sanctuary State

Dr. Alvaro Huerta

Date: March 21, 2017
Dear Governor Jerry Brown:

I propose for the State of California to become a sanctuary state, like the over 400 cities and counties around the country. According to Vanda Felbab-Brown of Brookings (January 31, 2017), sanctuaries, with some exceptions, don't cooperate with federal authorities on immigration-related issues: "These are areas that mostly do not cooperate with federal requests to hand over undocumented immigrants arrested by local police on unrelated charges, or where local police departments do not want to become an immigration enforcement body." While this may appear to be an extreme position for a state to take, it's not. It's based on the extreme reality of a rogue federal government, led by President Donald J. Trump and the GOP-controlled Congress, with its xenophobia agenda and draconian policies.

In this letter, I provide some reasons for Californian leaders to declare, via appropriate and legal means, a sanctuary state: (1) take a moral stance; (2) provide a concrete example for other states to resist federal government attacks against undocumented immigrants; (3) promote public safety, where undocumented immigrants can safely report true crimes without fear of deportation; and (4) protect vulnerable sanctuary cities and counties, where the federal government is threatening to withhold federal funds.

President Trump's anti-immigration executive orders take this country back to its dark past. This includes his executive order—signed on January 27, 2017—to ban individuals from Muslim-majority countries, including Syria, Iraq, Yemen, Sudan, Somalia, Iran and Libya. While Trump tries to frame this executive order as a national security measure, based on his own words from his presidential campaign, it's a Muslim ban.

Trump's other anti-immigration executive order—signed on January 25, 2017—focuses on sanctuary cities and counties. This order aims to punish sanctuary cities and counties by denying them federal funds for not cooperating with federal immigration agents. Like the Muslim ban, this order is framed as a public safety issue.

Given that California leads the country in providing undocumented immigrants with basic rights, like in-state tuition, driver's license and other measures, it makes sense for the state to counter Trump's xenophobic policies. By becoming a sanctuary state, California is taking a moral stance to protect vulnerable populations. As a result, California will encourage other states with Democratic governors to become sanctuary states by standing up for what's right.

As noted above, Trump frames his anti-immigrant executive orders as public safety measures, protecting the country from terrorists and criminals. To counter these false claims, immigration scholars' Wayne A. Cornelius, Angela S. García and Monica W. Varsanyi effectively argue in an insightful op-ed (*Los Angeles Times*, February 2, 2017) that sanctuary cities actually promote public safety, especially since immigrants feel safer to report crimes and potential criminal activity to law enforcement. Also, the scholars provide solid evidence that immigrants commit fewer crimes than the average American citizen.

By becoming a sanctuary state, California will protect existing sanctuary cities and counties. Instead of the Trump administration targeting vulnerable cities and counties with limited financial and legal resources, the state will provide the needed resources to protect these government entities. For example, on January 31, 2017, the City of San Francisco sued the Trump administration over its executive order against sanctuary cities. While it's great to see San Francisco leaders take a bold legal action to protect immigrants, why not have the state wage or join this lawsuit?

In terms of challenging Trump's threat to withhold funding from sanctuary entities, according to legal experts' Erwin Chemerinsky, Annie Lai and Seth Davis, in an excellent op-ed (*The Washington Post*, December 22, 2016), the law is on the side of the sanctuary entities, based on the Tenth Amendment and legal precedents, particularly *National Federation of Independent Business v. Seelius* (2012).

In short, by becoming a sanctuary state, California will prevail on legal and moral grounds.

THIRTY-FOUR

The "War on Immigrants"

Racist Policies in the Era of Trump

Dr. Alvaro Huerta

President Donald J. Trump's anti-immigration agenda centers on draconian, enforcement-based policies and executive orders, exacerbating an already dysfunctional immigration system. As an extension of Trump's presidential campaign, his administration's immigration policies also represent racist and xenophobic practices, such as anti-Mexicanism and Islamophobia. Like Trump's "Make America Great Again" campaign slogan, these immigration policies and orders promote an isolationist and a white nativist philosophy, hearkening back to the more oppressive and dark periods of U.S. history when racialized groups (e.g., Latinas/os, African Americans, Native Americans) lacked basic civil rights, privileges and freedoms under the law.

Complicating matters, Trump's immigration policies and orders are plagued with hyperboles and lies, making it difficult to differentiate between fact and fiction/fantasy (e.g., Mexico will "miraculously" pay for the border wall). However, while Trump has engaged in an ongoing "war on immigrants" campaign—in actions, words and tweets—against immigrants and their families/communities, a growing social movement of immigrant activists, immigrant advocates, scholars and elected officials have emerged to defend the civil and human rights of those who live and work in America's shadows.

On January 2, 1960, when then-Senator John F. Kennedy (JFK) announced his candidacy for President of the United States, the charismatic leader proclaimed: "The Presidency is the most powerful office in the

121

Free World. Through its leadership can come a more vital life for all of
our people. In it are centered the hopes of the globe around us for freedom and a more secure life . . ." (John F. Kennedy Presidential Library).
In contrast to JFK's aspirational announcement, on June 16, 2015, with his
immigrant wife by his side, then-presidential candidate Trump infa-
mously labeled Mexicans as "drug dealers," "criminals," and "rapists."
It's amazing how millions of Americans, mostly white folks, voted for
this racist idiot!

By targeting individuals of Mexican origin, Trump launched his presidential campaign on a racist political platform based on anti-Mexicanism—a long-standing American tradition embraced mostly by millions of
white citizens and voters. Trump's derogatory campaign also included
the creation of a "deportation force" (i.e., a military-style enforcement
apparatus) to detain, jail and deport millions of Mexicans, like the
government actions taken during 1950s with "Operation Wetback." During this racist program, the U.S. government deported over one million
Mexican immigrants, including Mexican Americans.

Similar to the inhumane internment camps of an estimated 120,000
Japanese immigrants and Japanese Americans during the 1940s, Trump's
immigration policies are intertwined with a long history of racism and
xenophobia in the U.S. This includes state-sponsored attacks against
Mexicans, Asians, Arabs (particularly Muslims) and other racialized
groups. Compared to European immigrants (particularly Northern and
Western Europeans of past generations), these racialized groups are also
viewed as inferior by leaders of the dominant culture. This is one of the
main arguments articulated by the late Dr. Samuel P. Huntington from
Harvard. That is, Trump and his administration didn't invent racist and
xenophobic policies or practices, since countless American leaders, prior
administrations and conservative scholars from the country's top universities have also demonized and scapegoated racialized immigrants
throughout U.S. history. For instance, during the late 1800s and early
1900s, immigrants from Southern and Eastern Europe, such as Italians,
Jews, Poles, Greeks and others, also experienced discrimination as ethnic
and religious groups (e.g., Catholic, Jewish).

Since the terrorist act of 9/11 (2001) on American soil, Arab immigrants and Arab Americans (particularly Muslims) have been targets of
racism in this country—more than usual. It's clearly evident to me and
other scholars that Trump's proposed Muslim ban during his presidential campaign represented a case of Islamophobia. Similarly, Islamophobia is also manifested in Trump's revised travel ban from the Muslim-
dominated countries, including Iran, Iraq, Libya, Somalia, Sudan, Syria
and Yemen. While the revised travel ban order excludes the word "Muslim," based on Trump's presidential candidacy (e.g., speeches, inter-
views), Trump is fulfilling a campaign promise to his "deplorable" supporters.

Moreover, while President Lyndon B. Johnson initiated the "war on poverty" and President Richard Nixon ignited the "war on drugs," Trump has championed the "war on immigrants." Trump's "war on immigrants" policies and rhetoric include demonizing Mexican immigrants, fantasizing over a stupid border wall (paid by U.S. tax-payers, not Mexico!), imposing a Muslim travel ban, targeting undocumented immigrants for deportation (regardless of criminal history) and other draconian proposals. Other draconian proposals include separating children from their parents when detained at the border and prosecuting individuals (e.g., parents, relatives) who pay human smugglers or *coyotes* to cross undocumented children into the U.S.

There's also a psychological component to the "war on immigrants," where Immigration and Customs Enforcement (ICE) agents are apprehending/arresting undocumented immigrants in places like courts and near schools, where immigration agents in the past have commonly ignored or respected as "safe" places. By doing so, the Trump administration is causing widespread panic among undocumented immigrants. Given that undocumented immigrants are not marginal or isolated actors, where they're embedded in communities and families/households that often include U.S. citizens (i.e., mixed-status households), Trump's "war on immigrants" campaign has also caused panic among Latinas/os, including Asian and Pacific Islanders and other groups with significant immigrant populations.

As part of a growing movement in response to these hostile federal actions, many elected officials across the country have joined in solidarity with undocumented immigrants, along with activists and advocates, in defying the Trump administration's racist and xenophobic policies. In California, state leaders and elected officials have filed lawsuits and taken legislative actions, such as considering "state sanctuary" measures.

During these turbulent and uncertain times for millions of immigrants (with or without legal status), it's imperative that we—those of us who believe in justice and dignity for all—advocate for humane and just policies for those on the margins, especially given their major contributions to this country on a daily basis.

THIRTY-FIVE

On the Chicana/o Moratorium of 1970 and the Case of Ruben Salazar

Dr. Juan Gómez-Quiñones

Some while ago, the upcoming fiftieth anniversary of the Chicana/o Moratorium (August 29, 1970) did loom in people's minds—memories have quickened since and so have questions. More than justifiable was the prominent front-page story of Eastern Group Publications (EPG), September 4, 2014, accompanied by an attention drawing sharp photograph of a ceremony celebrating a plaque commemorating the life of Ruben Salazar placed at Salazar Park in East Los Angeles. The volunteer ceremony, the modest plaque, the EGP story—all were commendable in several ways. Certainly commendable are these actions and words of those lighting this candle of memories.

To be sure, the memorial candle does not lighten either dark comers or as yet unwritten pages on all matters pertinent to the events of August 29, 1970. Indeed, the very heartening EGP story by a sensitive reporter who well may be a grandchild of those youth alive at the times of the August events, confesses there are questions to be asked even today, nearly fifty years later. Her questions inspire mine and more. They inspire the question, "What is our responsibility to her and the next generation, as we face the daunting memory of August 29, 1970, today when civil rights are at risk?"

Our grandparents have a saying our grandchildren should consider, "*mal pensar es asertar*"/"to think the worse is to be on the mark." Time passes for victims and culprits, but time does not heal all hurts. Moreover, time passages may second the intentions of culprits who prefer inattention or better forgetfulness of their crimes. As of yet, the misdeeds of the culprits of August 29th cannot achieve complete forgetfulness while witnesses live and, indeed, they do. Inevitably as days go by, eventually, there will be no witnesses to identify even redacted records to examine for scrutinous questioners to address. To some of us, some survivors of that day, the matters of August 29th are wounds demanding the need to be healed: "*una espina que se debe sanar.*" If we are consequent with rhetorical proclamations on the importance of history for future generations, then we must light the candle on the record written in the blood of those who died and those wounded on August 29, 1970.

On August 29th, civil rights were grossly and publicly violated. The films of the day clearly indicate this. Several credible persons including Stephanie Salazar Cook, Frank Sotomayor (*LA Observed*, August 27, 2010) and Hector Tobar (*Los Angeles Times*, July 9, 2010) have raised questions in print and persons. For instance, in addition to numerous sources, the film maker Phillip Rodriguez and the late journalist Frank del Olmo of the *Los Angeles Times* have indicated that the events of August 29th need clarification. The former-Los Angeles County Sheriff Lee Baca, once caretaker of the Sheriff's files on August 29th, has faced issues of his own on credibility (Court House News Service, May 12, 2017).

Matters of death caused by authoritarians and mass suppressions of civil rights by law authorities are serious questions of justice. Rather than simply describing, as usually done, at best and incompletely, the matters of August 29th—whether through print or camera—let us try to change how the facts and analyses of August 29th have been addressed and concluded. Given transitions within the L.A. County Board of Supervisors and the L.A. County Sheriff's Department, the time is more opportune than in the past to settle accounts on these matters. Quite clearly to some observers, the Supervisors, the Sheriff's Department and the District Attorney would not have endorsed an investigation in 1970.

Doing justice on August 29th matters at last could be achieved with an investigatory commission comprised of leading and experienced researchers whose combined work, according to professional history and law standards, culminates in a public report. Commission members would be persons eminently respected to civil rights efforts, law enforcement and judicial practices, such as Margaret E. Montoya (University of New Mexico Law), Lorena Oropeza (UC Davis), Laura E. Gómez (UCLA Law School), Ian Haney López (UC Berkeley Law), Edward Escobar (University of Arizona), and Ernesto B. Vigil (Independent Scholar). The commission could function through the auspices of MALDEF (Los Angeles) or the Center of Constitutional Rights (New York).

Necessary funding could be secured through the Office of a Los Angeles County Supervisor, which has discretionary funds at its disposal. Costs could be budgeted covering all operating expenses, including consultants, personnel, materials, travel, office needs, legal advisement, etc., for a period of two years. At a certain time, a report would be issued and the findings presented at community public hearings. Yes, a full investigation premised accounting is possible and the public should have an accounting, for the sake of all our civil rights. A full report would be in compliance in accordance with the pertinent amendments of the U.S. Constitution and the pertinent clauses of the California Constitution. All parties involved or associated would benefit the Sheriff's Department would be expected to be cooperative, when asked.

The intent of an investigatory commission and consequent report would be to do what has not been done—a full accounting. This means not subject to biased interference or influence by public offices or officers, of times past or now, and not subject to whims of public officials, past and current. Civil rights were violated in East Los Angeles nearly fifty years ago, just as surely as they were violated in the matter or police killing of Michael Brown and the suppression of democratic protests at Ferguson, Missouri, in 2014.

To date, a major cause of investigatory incompleteness on matters of August 29th is that no public office or official has claimed public responsibility for requiring and/or conducting a thorough investigation. How comforting for malfeasant doers, that in this case, neither some nearly fifty years ago nor today, there has been no public questioning, much less accounting. Baldly, such culprits argue there can be no investigation of possible crimes—their crimes. What glaringly stands out is that the actions of law enforcement were publicly committed and funded, but no one was or is in charge to accept responsibility for these actions.

There are August 29th basics that perforce are part of a complex people's history that may be subject to inquiry. Thus, there is a frame for the history of the tumultuous, and tragic events, and mendacious actions preceding, surrounding and following August 29th. Some struts of the frame would be as follows:

1. There needs to be a full appreciation of the qualitative dimensions of core and contextual elements of August 29th, not simply a quantitative assessment of these. The Chicana/o Moratorium was of significant importance to enforcement agencies, regionally and nationally, to act as they did. The attention given to it by law enforcement attests to that. Its importance at the time is reinforced by its recognized historical importance today. To be underscored is the fact August 29th constitutes a major civil rights and racist attack on the Mexican American community, not only with regional dimensions, but also with national implications. What comes to mind as a comparison with past mass suppressions of civil rights are the many oppressions and suppressions of Native Americans, as in the case of Wounded Knee, an ambush, resulting in casualties conducted by armed personnel acting under the cover of law.

2. The civil, political, economic, and cultural historical context of August 29th must be referred and spelled out specifically. August 29th is a culmination of the history of the consequences of repeated disregard for the political electoral under and misrepresentation of Mexican Americans, and the specific repeated violations of the civil rights of Mexican Americans and Mexicans in the greater Los Angeles area and Southern California region throughout the twentieth century. Moreover, here is a documented history of law enforcement practices and actions to be examined vis-à-vis minorities and labor organizing and community advocacies.

3. A public bona fide report would refer to these repressions and would include in its documentation references of public assaults on Mexican Americans which are recorded in scholarly works and in the rulings, finding the denial of voting and representational rights as evident in past court or administrative findings. Recall that as recent as 1990–1991, a court found Mexican Americans had been denied voting and representational rights in the Los Angeles area, such as *Garza v. County of Los Angeles* (1990–1991). The events of August 29th are consistent with a historical record that speaks volumes on injustices suffered by Mexican Americans.

4. The report would contextualize that the tragic events of August 29th which are parallel with analogous actions in the sixties and early seventies, whether in cities, rural areas or campuses of the United States.

5. What is to be explicitly noted, is whether there were extensive planning meetings on actions of one kind or another by police and intelligence agencies which, given the events of August 29th and subsequent actions, resulted in civil rights violations of residents and citizens. A key question is whether these meetings were in fact meetings that preceded the denial of civil rights of individuals. If so, whether the meetings were actions which ultimately led to deaths and injuries at the hands of law enforcement and to the arrests on counts of unsubstantiated charges of perhaps over a hundred individuals. The report would consider whether law officers (or other public officials) discussed actions that would lead to violations of civil rights of residents and citizens under cover of their office. Presumably, such "planning" as occurred could be considered engaging in conspiracy against the rights of citizens. The report would consider whether arrests and jailings would be discrete harmful actions done under the cover of law.

6. Moreover, if the Moratorium Committee was infiltrated prior to August 29th, as indicated in some of the literature, the why and wherefore of this would need to be examined and its infiltration related to events of August 29th. Infiltration is a planned action and it did occur; research literature and Federal Freedom of Infor-

mation documents indicate this. The Moratorium Committee is a party of some responsibility for its actions and inactions. Given its alleged infiltration, much before August 29th, this group needs to be examined as to internal workings that impacted the events of August 29th and its behavior before, during and immediately after the events.

7. As witnesses to the events of August 29th attest, there are several signs not least the massive staging and presence of law enforcement and equipment at several sites in proximity to the park, such actions indicate planning. Their presence alone subverted this march and an assembly. Thus, the matter of these planned preparations must be clarified. Too often, critical observers assume that what happens would follow top-down directives and thus there would be administrative documentation. In fact, the Sheriff's Department was internally complex and reportedly encompassed groups whose purpose and action presumably warranted secrecy by their participants, leaving scant or no paper trail.

8. No one has been critically questioned or cross-examined under oath on the actions of law enforcement and other officials in regards to matters of August 29th related to injuries and arrests. The so-called inquest hearing was a farce, as can be judged by the available film(s).

9. The physical behavior of law enforcement toward citizens and residents at the park assembly is plainly visible on film. This behavior has not been and should be addressed. The suppression of the assembly was brutal, as witnesses know and films show. The chaos visibly caused by officers served the purpose of providing ostensible grounds for mass arrests.

10. No one has addressed the facts that the death and injuries of individuals were promoted by law enforcement actions and that these also would constitute violations of human and civil rights. The peaceful assembly did not warrant these actions.

11. There were three publicly reported deaths. These deaths should be examined with equal attention. No one has addressed the fourth death of an individual associated with the activities of Barrio Alliance of Latin Americans (BALA) in the Santa Monica-Venice area and member of a known activist (Galvan family member) in this same area. Moreover, there is no adequate explanation as to why one body, that of Ruben Salazar, was unattended for an unreasonable length of time. If he had survived an initial shot, he would've had bled to death.

12. No one has raised the issue of civil rights violations given the possible targeting by law enforcement of the Denver-based Crusade for Justice members, in particular its leader, Rodolfo "Corky" Gonzales, who were visitors. Eventually, he and other Crusade

members were jailed on allegedly false charges. Why? Perhaps this targeting means planning for specific purposes not only related to Los Angeles. What were the possible purposes of this targeting and, if so, who would have ordered these purposes to fruition? Would and did this involve other agencies and does this involvement explain the lack of ready information available on the events of August 29th?

13. There are specific incidents that are telling of the larger mega scene which should be reported on. It should be noted that everyone involved on the participant side has stated that the march was festive and orderly, as was the assembly at the park. This is a noteworthy fact given what happened and how law enforcement rationalized part of their actions. Thus, the following are to be underscored:

- On the surface, a minor point: there is the presence of an ostensibly ultra-left group [not Community Part or Socialists Worker Party] parading with perfectly made signs, shouting their own slogans. Supposedly, they caused some commotion at the (south)west part of the park; though, this has never been explained by law enforcement. The group was not associated with the Moratorium organizing before, during or after the August 29th day. Their commotion supposedly served as the reason offered by some law enforcement to act initially at the (south)west margins of the crowd, according to some. Moreover, their presence provided bad-faith, pseudo-evidence for allegations of "commies" in this event, as voiced later by public officials and repeated by some spokespersons. Such allegations are a common ploy used by Los Angeles law enforcement for decades. They were mostly young white males, with short hair and preppie shirts and neat pants; their signs did not speak to the issues of the Moratorium. As far as anyone noted, they came and left untouched by law enforcement, even as the surrounding bedlam caused by law officers occurred. In effect, they received a pass. No law enforcement agents or media, then or later, questioned members of the group, though there are photos of them;
- Eventually, what law enforcement offered as reasons for their actions are events at a corner liquor store on Whittier Blvd. In some instances, law agents alleged the "owner" called them, concerning "pandemonium" at the store. Various participants, including persons at the store, have denied these allegations. In fact, there was no significant disorderliness at this corner store, which, in any case, was across the

street from the margins of the assembly. Why should the supposed store issue used by the police to attack the assembly? Without this false allegation, there would be no probable cause for disbursing and attacking the assembly. If something did occur at the store, as the police allege, why would a little customer impatience be a reason to shut down a lawful assembly of thousands? By the way, there is an implied racist stereotype here, as well as constitutional disregard;

- Next in the scenario of beginnings, supposedly law enforcement acted as they did because the crowd disobeyed blatantly an order to disburse. You would think such a dramatic announcement would be made by an appropriate officer at the stage of the assembly through the audio system there, or powerful police microphones would be used, meanwhile giving women and children time to leave in an orderly and safe way. No such initial order was heard by the front rows of the assembly; certainly not at the stage. Perhaps such order was not given to thousands, only whispered to a few. Perhaps the officers closest to the law enforcement speaker at the extreme (south)west edge of the assembly only mentioned to a few participants, or after police disbursement actions had begun. This questionable claim by officers served as a multi-purpose justification for their attack. Was this a misrepresentation or an outright lie by law enforcement leaders? Perhaps what followed from the alleged store incident and the unheard initial disbursement "order" represented reflections of poor training or simply incompetence by the Sheriff's Department? The officers who supposedly voiced orders that became the justification for terrorizing thousands, including women and children, and injuring hundreds, can be identified and questioned; they have not been. What happened during the assembly at the park has to be examined critically and separated and distinct from other matters of the 29th.

14. The matter of Ruben Salazar is both clearer and murkier than the actions directed at the assembly of August 29th. Moratorium Committee meetings were public, as well their participants. We must emphasize that Salazar's death is both linked and distinct from the hostility directed at the Moratorium Committee and subsequent assembly. Surely, and activists agree, the deaths of all on August 29th are equally tragic and presumably all are the responsibility of law enforcement personnel. Reportedly, Salazar was being monitored, so said his associates. If so, why? If freedom of information

(un-redacted) materials concerning the Moratorium and Ruben Salazar are fully available, would these documents indicate, clearly both were targeted? Presumably, the Moratorium mobilization and Salazar underwent, to some extent, distinct and discreet targeting, given that references to them occur in some files. Then-County Sheriff Lee Baca denied that Salazar was targeted (Robert J. Lopez, *Los Angeles Times*, February 19, 2011). Hundreds of pages of heavily redacted materials minimally tell the reader that assigned authorizes were monitoring community activities, organizations and spokespersons at the time. These doings are in themselves threats, arguably.

15. If there is evidence, written and oral, that Salazar was targeted, a question follows, why? Who is "they" behind the "why"? For what reasons, and who may be those who consciously targeted him? Quickly said is that they were not targeting Salazar to learn of places or persons of interest to him. "They" had that information, and, in any case, as a journalist in Los Angeles, his editors were aware of his activities and contacts. Salazar probably would have provided basic information on his journalist whereabouts, and on his reporting to his professional associates. Moreover, as media entities, the *Los Angeles Times* or KMEX Channel 34, if asked, would provide some or all of this information.

   • Probably, the political interest on Salazar was due to the possible consequences of his reporting through both English and Spanish media, nationally and internationally. To be sure, his reporting was not wholly on what he had to say about Mexican American East-siders in order to inform Los Angeles West-siders. His journalist concerns were cosmopolitan. Has there been obfuscation in regard to this outreach, part of which included the Latin American Left, by Latina/o media or writers to this day? The Leftist artist David A. Siqueiros understood his outreach, his art piece on him shows this;

   • An objective concern by Los Angeles influentials was perhaps because of Salazar's increasing knowledge of L.A. institutional insiders and their doings as a result of his interests and inquiries. He was linking the dots of Los Angeles City, Los Angeles County, institutional, corporate and electoral networks and, perhaps, beyond. Reportedly, he was informing himself on law enforcement institutions. Any number of sources will tell you how sensitive the powers that be were about on information on their inner workings during that era, so much under the public radar. As a journalist, Salazar had national and trans-national consequences and at certain juncture for a moment, so did the Moratorium;

- Salazar's professionalism, credibility and outreach in two language media systems were reportedly looked with askance by L.A. law enforcement and their backup politico networks. This was the Los Angeles of the 1950s and 1960s. Westside or eastside readers of the *Los Angeles Times* were not the major worry. This journalist had outreach beyond average L.A. newspaper readers, as important or more important than metropolitan reader outreach would be the collection of information by a competent credible professional in and of itself. As is known, journalists can be endangered by what they know as well as by what they have printed;

- For those underscored in Salazar's investigations, most probably they would seriously consider the significance of his journalist outreach. Imagine what Salazar would say about the events of August 29th and their aftermath if he was alive to report these, including explanatory references to the domestic unrest within the U.S., the populist opposition to the Vietnam War and so forth. Imagine to what extent his views on these would be picked up in and outside of Los Angeles in the U.S., and particularly in Latin America and in some parts of Europe. Remember, this was the world of the late sixties becoming the early seventies when critical journalists mattered;

- Salazar's politics, as can be attested, were moderate, on most domestic issues emphasizing fairness and equality. Salazar disavowed agitational rhetoric. He was not a man "stuck" in the middle, due to vague split loyalties or a person caught between some imagined contending sides within his profession nor was he a simple commercial bridge between language audiences or an affirmative action yuppie cautiously climbing an institutional ladder. He was a competent, forthright principled journalist. Clearly, if anything, he stood more firmly on his professional principles in 1970, as he had in the past. This ethical standing may have been perceived invidiously by those who imagined him as a threat;

- Investigatory research should explore that there are several mundane incidentals leading to Salazar's rendezvous with tragedy. A seasoned professional, he repeatedly confessed to friends that enemies may threaten him. He reported a visit to his office by two plain clothes individuals. Moreover, he, an experienced journalist having worked in Asia and Latin America where journalists were commonly under surveillance, believed he was being followed. If so, he would worry not so much about an information tracker but a target stalker. Such a stalker probably communicating by phone would have informed whomever on the other end of the line as to where Salazar was at any given moment. The stalker could have functioned as a spotter. Could this someone be part of the sidewalk traffic, a person making phone calls who could report where Salazar was at any given moment?;

- Supposedly, Ruben Salazar entered a Whittier Boulevard bar (Silver Dollar Bar) through a front doorway where persons stood, covered by a flapping curtain into a room with some light sufficient for customers to order and pay. Reportedly, some were leaving through the back. He sat at the bar, not seeing, not hearing? This was not a totally dark Silver Dollar. With commotion all around, immediately a special force appeared at the entrance with one individual presumably especially trained, especially armed, aiming this weapon at chest level at the bar, as photos show, not upward toward the ceiling. Who heard an order to disburse? Was one given?;

- As those who have followed the narratives, there are on these actions known, the law enforcement statements can be examined for contradictions and absences; and certainly as to what supposedly happened, such statements are contradicted by several witnesses including media persons: why and what happened and why and how did Salazar die or killed?

- Little is known about the supposed shooter. A respected Los Angeles urban scholar has told listeners that the deputy described as a rookie by law enforcement and inquest staff had an aggressive past vis-à-vis Mexican Americans in relation to a labor/protest dispute(s). This allegation contradicts his claimed and proffered inexperience by the Sheriff's Department. Moreover, the official rationale for using a fly-rite missile weapon (somewhat like a dated grenade launcher) into a room with humans is preposterous, as is the claim of total darkness in the bar and a heavy curtain impeding the view of an entire squad of police officers. (Or, was it indeed a flapping curtain as photos show?). Presumably, arguably the shooter did not see his shot hit. Indeed, a trained officer shoots into a darkened space, if true, and into a space where persons are reported present, if true?

An investigatory committee has a chilling but doable task. If this is an accidental death, its reporting should have been dealt with quickly and openly. To date, the questions and suspicions have arisen are done in part due because of lack of credible bona fide public hearing on an important public matter, his and our civil rights.

Furthermore, there are several aspects to be noted in the aftermath of August 29th. What motivation set off the Moratorium clash and actions setting off the Silver Dollar death of Salazar and the deaths of others are as yet not satisfactorily explained. Why are there so many loose ends? The inquest was a farce, compare it to the victim Latasha Harlins' investigations of yesterday or any death by an officer on duty today. The whole scene of what supposedly took place in the Silver Dollar is questionable in several aspects. What about the exit back of the bar? What happened to the supposed presence of an armed man that served as justification and probable cause for law enforcement at the bar? If true, was he in the bar with Salazar? An armed man missing? A hoax? If people were leaving, why did Salazar not leave? Was the autopsy thorough? Was the weapon and its various munitions examined by an independent expert?

The fact remains there was reckless use of a destructive weapon, resulting in the death of an acclaimed and recognizable journalist by supposedly a trained officer following orders. Who gave the orders? Or, again, is there an order claimed to be given to clear the area of the Silver Dollar and/or not heard by anyone other than officers? If so, why would Salazar or others at the bar not hear it? Who did fire the fatal shot? What if, actually, someone fully or partially inside the bar fired the lethal shot?

Certainly, officers at the scene have not been questioned under oath by independent counsel. Amazingly, no one has raised the question whether the officers who admitted being at the shooting were assisted by special personnel or supervised at the site by higher-ups. Is there a "patsy" here? On the August 29th matter, if no one has effectively been questioned, and an "official" explanation has been unquestioned, therefore, why would a guilty person feel accountable or apprehensive? Why would any informed person come forth then? Why would anyone involved with the law or judiciary side feel the need to change a story that exonerates him and everyone else in the story? Once that story became publicly official and publicly endorsed, it thus became officially inviolate.

If the official story is so solid, why the cover-up for decades? Why not answering questions? Why the delay? Why did it take a reporter's filing forty years later for some minor redacted material to be available? The fact is that a cover-up, when it occurs, is a fact. What kind of reporting and editorializing would Salazar have written if he had survived the August 29th tragedy of a massive assault on a peaceful assembly in a Mexican American neighborhood? Who would he hold responsible for the events of August 29th?

Perhaps the matters are given substance beyond aftermath questions by the irrefutable fact that the matters of August 29th and Salazar have not been clarified to this day. If there is nothing to hide on the matter, why make clarity on them difficult for nearly fifty years? Quite conveniently for facilitating this cover-up is that there is no one empowered, we are told, to be a doer and mover in exacting responsibility. However, there is initiative to safeguard institutional personnel and, thus, cohesion.

Few over the age of reason will believe that district attorney representatives, sheriff's officials or police chiefs or law enforcement agencies will volunteer to investigate themselves. However, there are forensic cold case investigations that work, and yield results. There are newspapers reports on these matters. "Murder will out" is an old English saying. This August 29th, the door remains shut. Here, no one wants to bite this spent bullet.

Obviously, why "they" don't explain is in part why the matter remains un-clarified. Thus, this obfuscation is why the matter calls for independent investigation with power of public credibility and professional questioning of witnesses and the issuing of a credible public report subject to public scrutiny. Seeking the truth is positive for all, not negative.

If events and personages of August 29th are public history worthy of being memorialized at a public park, as public education, so be it. If this story is worthy of inclusion in public education, the Superintendent office of the LAUSD that has contacts with major education materials and technology corporations could ask them for costs to sustain an investigation and its conclusions included in text books, etc., for students. Perhaps LAUSD would say this matter may be history, but it is not within their scope. The report may not answer all questions, but raising civil rights related questions would be a worthwhile set of lessons in these days when civil rights must be upheld.

More to the immediate point is for a County Supervisor to initiate or encourage an appropriate history focused investigation. From his or her district funds, he or she could fund such an investigation or to publicly support such an investigation by calling on select donors for funding. To be willing to fund a professional and comprehensive investigation by bona fide scholars under the auspices of one or more prestigious civil rights organizations is civically meritorious. Alongside an investigation endorsed by a board member or members, there are other investigatory alternatives provided there are funds. For example, independent of a public official, a civil rights organization can name a committee of legal and history scholars to conduct an investigation and issue a public report. Perhaps a university research center or program can collaborate. The point for all is to defend civil rights.

If we are willing to commemorate these August 29th memorable events, we should accept the further challenge of upholding civil rights for all including the residents of East Los Angeles and the activists of August 29th—actions that undeniably happened on the watch of the Los Angeles County Board of Supervisors. The Acoma Pueblo of New Mexico, through its governing council, commemorates an injustice endured 500 years ago. We can do something more modest, shine a candle on dark comers of major violations of civil rights that occurred in Los Angeles County on August 29, 1970.

Thereupon, we say with the Mourner's Kaddish, "May there be abundant peace from heaven, and life for us . . . to which we say Amen."

THIRTY-SIX

Advocating for the Immigrant Domestic Workforce

Dr. Alvaro Huerta

City leaders, urban planners and architects plan livable communities for the public. But these plans often exclude the low-wage workers who carry out the domestic household services in mostly middle-class and affluent communities. This work force includes those who clean our homes, take care of our children, repair our homes and maintain our yards. These workers—many of them immigrants and racialized minorities—are not well represented in the political or planning process.

The bureaucratic planning process commonly fails to provide adequate public transportation for nannies and housecleaners, who toil inside suburban homes and gated communities. In addition, planners typically don't solicit feedback or input from paid Latino gardeners when designing and creating suburban front yards—an American obsession. Meanwhile, many immigrant workers lack the time, language skills and educational background to have a voice in the formal planning process.

The immigrant domestic household economy encompasses housecleaners, day laborers and paid gardeners. This informal workforce—mostly Latina/o immigrants in California and beyond—has taken over the traditional household duties and responsibilities that many Americans assumed before WWII, when women regularly stayed home to care for their children and cleaned the house, while men worked outdoors to "master" the front lawn of the archetypal suburban home.

Due to their limited English skills, low educational background and lack of financial capital, most recent immigrants seek low-wage jobs, which Americans have come to reject due to their dismal pay, bleak opportunities and low social status (e.g., "immigrant jobs," "dirty jobs"). Most of these so-called immigrant jobs require intense manual labor and pose workplace hazards. While Latina immigrants primarily work as nannies and housecleaners in this informal sector, like my late mother, Latino immigrants dominate the paid gardening niche, like my late-father-in-law, and day labor workforce, particularly in the Southwestern states.

According to conservative voices, recent immigrants from Mexico and elsewhere are unproductive and dangerous individuals, representing social burdens and national security threats to this country. Immigrant workers, they argue, come to the United States to seek government assistance, bring drugs, commit crimes, take away jobs from native workers, depreciate wages and pose dangers to society.

These claims can be easily refuted. Immigrants without legal status, for instance, have been barred from receiving governmental assistance under former President Bill Clinton's 1996 Personal Responsibility and Work Opportunity Reconciliation Act of 1996 (or Welfare Reform Act of 1996). Thus, how can immigrants represent a government or economic drain when they don't qualify for federal programs and services? Moreover, while conservatives argue that immigrants commit more crimes than U.S. citizens, they rarely provide any hard data to substantiate their claims.

On the contrary, recent research shows that undocumented immigrants, on average, commit less crime than American citizens, especially once we consider age, gender and other factors to make valid comparisons. To make accurate comparisons, for instance, we need to compare apples to apples and oranges to oranges. Given that that recent immigrants are younger (and most likely male) compared to American citizens, then we can't compare these two groups equitably when it comes to crime. This is important because we know that younger individuals are more likely to commit crimes than older individuals. In his insightful essay, "His-Panic: The Myth of Immigrant Crime," published in *The American Conservative* magazine (March 2010), the conservative Ron Unz does an excellent job of examining the complex nature of immigration vis-à-vis crime rates. He analyzes existing data to debunk myths perpetuated by conservatives and others about the so-called Latina/o immigrant menace. Despite being a leading force against bilingual education in California in the 1990s, Unz finally puts his elite educational background (Harvard and Stanford) to some good use by closely examining the nuances of crime rates in the United States. In short, Unz argues that Latino immigrants commit less crimes than white citizens.

In addition to anti-immigrant public debates, many local public policies directly target the immigrant workforce. We can clearly see an example of anti-immigrant legislation in the City of Los Angeles' leaf blower ban of the mid-1990s. On December 3, 1996, the city council voted by a

9–3 margin to ban gas-powered leaf blowers in residential areas. The draconian penalties for using this work device, operated mainly by Latino gardeners, included a misdemeanor charge, $1,000 fine, and up to six months in jail. In response, Latino gardeners, with the support of Chicana/o activists, where I played a key leadership role (as previously noted), founded the Association of Latin American Gardeners of Los Angeles (ALAGLA). As a result, ALAGLA initiated one of the most dynamic social justice movements since the United Farm Workers (UFW) and Chicana/o Movement during the 1960s and 1970s.

Following countless protests, marches, press conferences, candlelight vigils and a week-long hunger strike, the Latino gardeners (and Chicana/o activists) eventually prevailed, forcing the city council to dramatically amend this law. While the affluent Westside residents who favored the ban focused on "public nuisance" aspects of leaf blowers, such as noise and air pollution, the Latino gardeners (and Chicana/o activists) successfully re-framed the issue as the "haves against the have-nots." Eventually, the ALAGLA prevailed in the court of public opinion and successfully managed to defeat the draconian aspects of this ordinance.

Another example of anti-immigrant legislation includes Arizona's SB 1070, requiring enforcement authorities to question anyone they "suspect" of lacking legal status in the United States. In addition, some municipalities are passing laws that allow building owners to seek proof of citizenship from renters. Given that immigration enforcement pertains to the jurisdiction of the federal government, these laws have been successfully challenged in the courts. Nevertheless, the anti-immigrant hysteria in this country has generated an atmosphere of fear and harassment for the more than 11 million undocumented immigrants in this country.

Despite lacking higher education, special training and financial capital, many immigrant workers and petty-entrepreneurs are sophisticated individuals who own and operate their own small businesses. Latino gardeners, for example, regularly engage in complex entrepreneurial transactions, such as expanding business operations, developing client routes, billing and receiving, trading goods and services with other small businesses.

Apart from being business savvy, Latino gardeners make our communities greener, cleaner, safer and more beautiful. While not recognized for it, they also increase property values. They also relieve middle-class and affluent individuals from performing time-consuming and labor-intensive yardwork.

To meet the needs of the indispensable immigrant workforce, city leaders, planners and architects should accommodate domestic household service workers when designing, creating, and redeveloping communities. For example, do wealthy communities have access to public transportation for nannies and housecleaners? Do planners and policy makers pressure and provide incentives for manufacturers of gas-powered leaf blowers and other gardening work devices to produce quiet, environmentally friendly equipment?

In the spirit of the late planning theorist and practitioner, Paul David-off, planners should resurrect the advocacy-planning model and directly meet the needs of immigrants and racialized minorities who lack the political clout and financial capital to defend themselves against unjust laws and policies. In the advocacy planning model, planners take on the role of a lawyer by advocating for immigrant and marginalized commu-nities to meet their specific needs in city hall and beyond. Generally speaking, planners and architects have remained silent in challenging claims that recent immigrants are to blame for high crime rates, depleted social services and increased poverty. There are exceptions, however, like myself and others.

When creating and advocating for greener communities, such as building more parks and planting more trees in urban areas, planners and architects should promote the role of immigrant workers and petty-entrepreneurs as part of this important mission. Instead of criminalizing Latino gardeners, as in the case of the City of Los Angeles' leaf blower ban, planners and architects should work closely with policy makers and concerned community members to create alternative solutions for all par-ties, including the immigrant work force that takes on the most difficult and least respected jobs in America.

To sum, in America's cities, suburbs and rural areas, urban planners and architects represent the ideal actors to plan, communicate and advo-cate on behalf of *los de abajo*/those on the bottom.

THIRTY-SEVEN

President Barack Obama Should've Halted Mass Deportations

Dr. Alvaro Huerta

During his time in office, then-President Barack Obama should've halted his mass deportation policy. Surpassing his predecessors, Obama deported over 2.7 million undocumented immigrants. He also doubled down on harsh enforcement measures toward undocumented immigrants, such as close collaboration among employers, local officials and Immigration and Customs Enforcement (ICE) agents. Undocumented immigrants have been organizing against such policies for many years (to the present). Not satisfied with receiving temporary relief under the 2012 Deferred Action for Childhood Arrivals (DACA) program, for example, undocumented immigrant youth, or DREAMers, have demanded relief for their parents, too.

In solidarity with the undocumented youth and their families, on March 2, 2014, Janet Murguia, president of the National Council of La Raza (NCLR), a prominent Latina/o advocacy group, characterized Obama as the "Deporter-in-Chief," demanding that the president take unilateral action to halt deportations. Let's not forget that NCLR previously echoed Obama's draconian principles on immigration reform, such as militarization of the U.S.-Mexico border, employer sanctions, stringent measures fines and back taxes on aspiring citizens. In speaking out against Obama's mass deportations, Murguia finally expressed the frustrations and demands of undocumented immigrants and their advocates. (Founded in 1968, on July 10, 2017, NCLR announced a major name change to UnidosUS.)

This one act by Murguia represented trouble not only for Obama in particular, but also for Democrats in general. Obama wasted no time in defending himself as the "Champion-in-Chief" of immigration reform. Latinas/os know "I've got their back," he asserted. But with his inhumane record on immigration not much different from Republicans, Latinas/os were torn about their electoral loyalties. Imagine if Obama didn't have "the back" of Latinas/os?

In a period of dramatic demographic change in this country, it's about time for Latinas/os to flex their political and economic clout by invoking their basic human rights and demanding to be treated with dignity and respect. Instead of accepting draconian immigration reform plans from Democrats and Republicans that exclude many or all of estimated eleven undocumented immigrants from a pathway toward citizenship, this large and heterogeneous group should always demand what immigrants deserve and earn on a daily basis: amnesty.

While in office, Obama could've redeemed himself with Latinas/os, yet he didn't. How could he turn his back on a key voting bloc that helped get him elected, twice? He should've exercised his executive privileges by halting deportations and supporting Latina/o immigrants.

Speaking of supporting Latina/o immigrants, if Democrats expect Latinas/os to support them in future elections, especially in 2020 to recapture the White House from the "Hustler-in-Chief" and Senate from the morally bankrupt Republican leaders, Democrats must advocate for and guarantee immediate relief to millions of undocumented immigrants living and working in America's shadows.

THIRTY-EIGHT

Demanding a Clean DACA Bill, Now!

Dr. Alvaro Huerta

Democratic leaders should unite and stand firm against President Donald J. Trump—the "Hustler-in-Chief"—and the complicit Republican leaders on passing a clean immigration bill on DACA. A clean bill only focuses on DACA (Deferred Action for Childhood Arrivals), which provides temporary protections from deportation and work permits for an estimated 800,000 young undocumented immigrants. Implemented by former President Barack Obama—or the "Deporter-in-Chief"—as an executive order on June 15, 2012, Trump announced the phase out of DACA on September 5, 2017. As a manufactured crisis created by Trump, unless Congress acts or the courts successfully intervene on behalf of the participating immigrants, DACA will end on March 5, 2018, creating havoc for hundreds of thousands of undocumented youth and their families. More specifically, if the Trump administration and Congress prevail, the violent Immigration and Customs Enforcement (ICE) agents or *la migra* will begin to target the energetic, productive and hard-working undocumented youth with mass deportations.

I was originally skeptical of DACA, since I didn't trust government officials, self-serving politicians or Obama—who, despite his eloquence and brilliance, deported an estimated 2.7 million undocumented immigrants—with the personal data (e.g., names, addresses) of so many undocumented youth who applied, facilitating mass deportations by future administrations, such as the racist Trump administration. That said, as a U.S.-born citizen and scholar where I freely exercise my First Amendment rights without fear of state repression (it might still occur!), I can't chide the undocumented youth who desperately sought/seek temporary protections to live, work and pursue higher education without the terror of *la migra* following their every move.

I don't know what it feels like to be in a constant state of fear or anxiety, not knowing when *la migra* will deport me (or my parents) at any given day. (Actually, I did grow up in public housing projects, where I experienced the horrors of poverty, state violence and hopelessness, but that's another story.) For undocumented immigrants, it's not just *la migra*; it's also the police. In non-sanctuary municipalities, the police and local authorities often comply with *la migra*, where a simple traffic violation could easily lead to detention and deportation.

Moreover, *la migra* also targets undocumented immigrants at court hearings and near schools. Apparently, even racist companies like Motel 6 and managers are complicit by sharing their guest lists of "Latino sounding names" with *la migra*. In my old barrio, two words describe those who cooperate with repressive authorities: cowardly snitches!

While undocumented immigrants and their allies continue to organize against the racist Trump administration and complicit Republican leaders, Democratic leaders, who depend on the Latina/o vote, have failed miserably. For instance, when Michael Wolff's explosive book, *Fire and Fury: Inside the Trump White House*, had Trump "on the ropes" by portraying him as child-like, dumb, unfit, unstable, irrational, incoherent, narcissistic, disloyal, dishonest, womanizer, absentee father and other unfavorable traits for the most powerful man in the world, Democratic leaders went ahead and met with Trump and Republican leaders on January 9, 2018, to discuss so-called immigration reform. This included Sen. Dianne Feinstein (D-CA), Sen. Mazie Hirono (D-HI), Rep. Steny Hoyer (D-MD) and Rep. Henry Cuellar (D-TX). Televised and moderated by Trump—who, despite contradicting himself repeatedly and displaying his gross ignorance on immigration policy in front of the media—he was able to change the national discourse away from Wolff's insightful and explosive book. Obviously, the complicit media or state-controlled media (i.e., Fox News) played along, once again, with Trump's opportunistic photo op.

What's wrong with the Democratic leaders in Congress? Maybe being in the same room with a "moron" like Trump—to use Secretary of State Rex Tillerson's alleged description of his boss—has rubbed off on them? Instead of meeting with Trump and Republican leaders who had a list of pre-conditions to support DACA, such as funding a medieval wall, ending family re-unification policies (so-called "chain migration") and terminating the diversity visa system, the Democratic leaders should've demanded their own pre-condition, such as a clean DACA bill!

While Trump lied, like he usually does, about respecting and accepting any immigration bill proposal that resulted from this flawed bi-partisan meeting, in another White House-led immigration meeting (January 11, 2018)—with only one Democratic Senator in attendance, Sen. Richard J. Durbin (D-IL), according to *The Washington Post* (January 12, 2018) and confirmed by Sen. Durbin (January 12, 2018)—Trump displayed his true colors about black and brown immigrants by referring to El Salvador, Haiti and African countries, as "shithole countries." This racist and grotesque statement provides us with Trump's underlying rationale for his draconian immigration policies. This includes ending the temporary protected status (TPS) for immigrants from Nicaragua (November 6, 2017), Haiti (November 20, 2017) and El Salvador (January 8, 2018). While Trump dreams about deporting brown and black immigrants, replacing them with European immigrants from countries like Norway, it's time for all Democratic leaders to unite and stand firm against Trump's racist agenda and the complicit Republican Party.

Democratic leaders must learn from their counterparts, like when Republican leaders obstructed then-President Obama's progressive agenda—actually, not all of it was progressive, like deporting over 2.7 undocumented immigrants and deploying murderous drones in majority-Muslim countries. By refusing to collaborate with the nation's first African American president, Republican leaders successfully blocked Obama's Supreme Court Justice nominee, Judge Merrick B. Garland. ("Thanks" to their obstructionism, Trump's reactionary Supreme Court Justice Neil M. Gorsuch with his reactionary legal views will be playing a key role on the highest court in the land for many years.) Thus, Democratic leaders must learn to play hardball with Trump.

For Democratic leaders, the goal should be that Trump fails to advance his racist, xenophobic and pro-corporate political agenda, like funding for his stupid wall (that Mexico will never pay for!), deporting undocumented immigrants in mass, providing tax breaks for the rich, deregulating industry and destroying our environment.

Finally, Democratic leaders should cultivate and advance viable, progressive candidates to take over the Senate and House in this year's midterm elections. By doing so, Democratic leaders will check Trump's xenophobic and co-corporate agenda by building a political wall between Congress and the White House. Thus, by opposing Trump's funding for his stupid wall and other draconian immigration measures, the Democrats will most likely win the White House in 2020.

THIRTY-NINE

No Deal on "Sh*thole" Border Wall!

Dr. Alvaro Huerta

If Democratic leaders make a deal with President Donald J. Trump on his "sh*thole" border wall, they will guarantee his re-election in 2020. (Here, I'm borrowing the word "shithole" from the self-proclaimed "stable genius" in the White House.) Eight years of a disastrous Trump administration is not acceptable! Neither the United States nor the world can survive eight years of the "Hustler-in-Chief."

It appears that Special Counsel Robert Mueller's ongoing investigation represents our only hope to impeach Trump or force him to resign, following in the footsteps of former President Richard M. Nixon. (I hope you don't feel any pressure, Mr. Mueller, since the country and world depend on you!) And while he's at it, Mueller shouldn't forget about Vice President Mike Pence—a more polished bigot and hustler.

Regarding funding for his "sh*thole" wall, let's not forget that Trump, during his presidential campaign, guaranteed his rabid and "deplorable" supporters that Mexico will pay for it. When Mexican leaders rebuked his white-nationalist fantasy, Trump, in a GOP primary debate on CNN (February 25, 2016), responded with a false sense of indignity: "The wall just got ten feet higher."

If Trump was mostly elected on the racist premise to restrict brown people (and Muslims) from entering the United States, then, why are Democratic leaders negotiating with Trump on providing funding for his "sh*thole wall"? According to *The Washington Post* (January 20, 2018), Senate Minority Leader Charles E. Schumer (D-NY) originally offered Trump funding for the "sh*thole" wall in exchange for Trump's support of DACA (Deferred Action for Childhood Arrivals).

It's disappointing, but not surprising, that even Rep. Luis Gutiérrez (D-IL)—as a so-called advocate of immigrants in Congress—also offered to support Trump's "sh*thole" wall in exchange for DACA. According to Gutiérrez, in an interview on CNN (January 20, 2018), in order to help DACA recipients or DREAMers, he's willing to "go down there [U.S.-Mexico border] with bricks and mortar and begin the wall." If this actually occurs, once completed, Gutiérrez should stay on the south side of the border!

What's wrong with Schumer and Gutierrez? Don't they understand that if Trump secures billions of dollars for his "sh*thole" wall—his signature campaign promise—he'll keep his major campaign promise, securing his re-election in 2020!

As I've previously argued, Trump manufactured a crisis among DACA recipients when on September 5, 2017, he announced the end of this program—an executed order by then-President Barack Obama to provide temporary relief from deportation and work permits for an estimated 800,000 undocumented youth. As the "Hustler-in-Chief," Trump is now using DACA as a bargaining chip to secure his "sh*thole" wall.

Now that Schumer has come to his senses (or was pressured to do so) by withdrawing his support for Trump's "sh*thole" wall—after caving on the three-day government shutdown—the Senate Minority Leader and fellow Democrats in Congress must unite and stand firm against the "Racist-in-Chief" and complicit Republican leaders to pass a clean DACA bill.

Following the example of Republican leaders, Democratic leaders must be on the same page and use the same talking points in framing their argument for DACA in particular and comprehensive immigration reform in general. For instance, in framing their case and acting in unison, Republican leaders are advancing a xenophobic and an enforcement-only immigration agenda by ending the diversity visa lottery program, terminating family-reunification (so-called "chain migration"), securing funding for the "sh*thole" wall and promoting other draconian measures, like E-Verify.

To counter these extremist positions, Democratic leaders should forcefully argue—without compromise—that Trump and the morally bankrupt Republican leaders don't want any more brown or black people migrating to this country. During a White House-led meeting on January 11, 2018, when inquiring about immigrants from El Salvador, Haiti and African countries, Trump revealed his true "motives" behind his thinking (assuming he thinks for himself) on immigration policies: "Why are we having all these people from shithole countries come here?"

To get on the offensive, Democratic leaders should repeatedly ask Trump and the complicit Republican leaders if they only care about immigrants from European countries, like Norway? Moreover, by countering Trump and the deplorable GOP, Democratic leaders should frame the current immigration debate on just and humane principles. This includes basic principles, such as: we should recognize that no human being is "illegal"; we should value diversity; we should build bridges versus walls; and we should advocate for unity versus division.

Furthermore, in defending immigrants, Democratic leaders should reject false dichotomies, such as the "good immigrant" versus the "bad immigrant" paradigm. In the case of DACA or DREAMers, as part of a false dichotomy, undocumented youth represent "good immigrants" (e.g., "arrived in this country at no fault of their own") and their parents symbolize "bad immigrants" (e.g., "law breakers who must be punished").

Enough with this nonsense!

To be better equipped—strategically and intellectually—to challenge Trump and the immoral Republican leaders, it behooves Democratic leaders to read Dr. George Lakoff's brilliant book on values and frames, *The ALL NEW Don't Think of an Elephant!: Know Your Values and Frame the Debate*. They should also read Dr. Michael Dear's excellent book against border walls, *Why Walls Won't Work: Repairing the US-Mexico Divide*. This includes Dr. Dear' insightful op-ed, "Mr. President, Tear Down This Wall," in *The New York Times* (March 10, 2013). Additionally, Democratic leaders should view Dr. Bridget Anderson's inspiring 2011 TEDx talk, "Imagining a World Without Borders." Moreover, apart from my first book, *Reframing the Latino Immigration Debate: Towards a Humanistic Paradigm*, I highly recommend that Democrats view my 2015 TEDx talk, "Migration as a Universal Human Right."

Finally, while Democratic leaders must redeem themselves on the question of immigration—based on their unjust and inhumane record of supporting draconian policies and programs—it's incumbent on all of us—those who believe in just and humane immigration reform—to advocate for and collaborate with those living and working in America's shadows.

FORTY

Viva the Scholar-Activist!

Dr. Alvaro Huerta

I am a Chicano scholar-activist.

What does it mean for me to be a scholar-activist? (Thanks for asking.) Based on my understanding, it means that I have one foot in the academy or academe and one foot in Chicana/o-Latina/o communities. It means being a bridge between these asymmetric spaces: institutions of higher education and racialized/working-class communities. It means for the former, with its privileged members, to serve the latter—not vice versa, as is the norm.

As an interdisciplinary scholar, I have been trained or socialized to the norms and rules of the academy. This includes earning advanced degrees from elite universities. I say this not to boast or brag (well, maybe a little bit!), but to push back against everyone who has questioned my academic abilities—as a former Chicano kid from the projects in East Los Angeles—to compete and thrive in higher education. While I am not seeking pity or sympathy—especially given my privileged positionality—too often, similar to my violent upbringing, I must regularly defend myself against academic bullies and haters—to put it in scholarly terms.

A message to the academic bullies and haters: I am not a Mexican boy to be pushed around or patted on the head! So, as the brilliant Kendrick Lamar raps, "Sit down . . . "

Higher education is like mountain climbing: the higher you climb, the whiter it gets. This is one reason why so many Chicana/o graduate students and faculty members experience a sense of isolation and alienation in elite white spaces. As one of the few Chicana/o urban planning faculty members in the country, throughout my graduate studies and academic career, I have often been the only brown body in the room. While I do not get intimidated by anyone or any situation, especially since I survived the mean streets of East Los Angeles, I aim to change this unjust reality in the academy. Actually, since my undergraduate years at UCLA, I've been advocating for more working-class Chicanas/os, Latinas/os and other racialized groups to pursue higher education.

As a faculty member and public intellectual, I am in a position to help more people from similar backgrounds like mine to get ahead: racialized minorities, children of immigrants, first-generation university students, working-class background, violent upbringings and so on. I especially encourage historically marginalized youth to not only seek undergraduate degrees, but also to pursue graduate and professional degrees. This includes speaking at high schools, community colleges and community forums. This also includes organizing on-campus workshops on demystifying the application process for graduate and professional schools. We desperately need more faculty members, regardless of racial and class background, to do likewise!

When it comes to serving or advocating for Chicana/o communities and other racialized groups, while many faculty members "talk a good game," they don't "walk the talk." Like the concept of the rational actor — which means that individuals act in their self-interest — these individuals are more interested in advancing their own social and professional status than to help foster the next generation of scholars. While I am not against the idea of individual advancement, I am against individuals who purposely exploit racialized and working-class communities — by extracting their knowledge, lived experiences, stories, etc. — to advance their own research agendas and professional goals without any form of reciprocation.

In my case, not only did I grow up poor, but I also spent over thirteen years as a community organizer before pursuing my graduate studies. In doing so, I incurred opportunity costs. In other words, instead of advancing my professional career, like many of my peers and colleagues, I invested my time and energy in defending and serving marginalized communities. Among other actions, as previously noted, this included: leading a grassroots campaign to defeat a proposed power plant in the City of South Gate, California (early 2000s); co-organizing Latino immigrant gardeners against a draconian law in the City of Los Angeles (late 1990s); and co-organizing a hunger strike by five Chicana/o students at UCLA to defend financial aid support and other services for undocumented students (mid-1980s).

In fact, the UCLA hunger strike in 1987, which I helped organize as a member of MEChA (*Movimiento Estudiantil Chicano de Aztlán*) , represented a precursor to a similar action led by Chicana/o students (and one faculty member) on this same campus in 1993. The 1993 hunger strike eventually facilitated the creation of the César E. Chávez Department of Chicana and Chicano Studies. This department has helped the university to create more ethnic studies and social justice classes for its Chicana/o-Latina/o student population. It has also facilitated the hiring of Chicana/o-Latina faculty members. Many years later, I am still waiting for my Hallmark "thank-you card" or See's Candies box from both the department and university! Since campus activism and community organizing efforts consist of collective efforts by dedicated individuals and leaders, we should always give credit to everyone involved in any cause for social, racial and economic justice. That said, all of my social justice victories derived from collective efforts of like-minded individuals with a singular goal of helping the marginalized.

The scholar-activist, like the late comedian Rodney Dangerfield's self-deprecating humor, gets no respect in the academy. While traditional or mainstream scholars refuse to fully recognize our research-action efforts, activists criticize us for operating in the so-called Ivory Tower. This is a reality or predicament that Chicanas/os (Mexican-Americans) are all too familiar with. That is, Chicanas/os are not "Mexican enough" for "real Mexicans" from the motherland and not "American enough" for white Americans in *el norte*. To deal with this reality or resolve this predicament, both scholar-activists and Chicanas/os must accept their/our distinct identities with pride and determination, regardless of what others think of them/us.

While I accept the "publish or perish" mantra in the academy, I always publish without losing sight of my ultimate object: to improve the lives of historically marginalized communities. This is where I separate myself from traditional or mainstream academics, who falsely believe that only publishing esoteric articles in peer-reviewed journals will bring about the necessary structural changes to improve or transform the lives of immigrants, racialized groups and working-class communities. While I also publish in peer-reviewed journals and university presses, like Dr. Helen Sword posits, I aim to write "clearly and engagingly" in my both academic and public scholarship for the public good.

In addition to academic publications, I strongly believe that institutions of higher education—both teaching and research oriented—should give credit (e.g., tenure and promotion) to faculty members who engage in public scholarship with non-refereed articles, essays and policy papers. Given that only a small fraction of peer-reviewed articles get read due to restricted access, more people have access to non-refereed publications, given their availability and accessible language. This is especially the case for publications with positive impacts in (re)framing arguments and public policies to advance progressive agendas in this country and beyond. It is also the case for advancing action-based research findings in widely accessible periodicals and reports to improve the lives of *los de abajo*/those on the bottom.

In short, I unconditionally endorse what a wise German philosopher wrote almost 175 years ago, applicable to all academic fields: "Philosophers have hitherto only interpreted the world in various ways; the point is to change it."

FORTY-ONE

In Memory of My Beloved Brother

Noel "Nene" Huerta

Dr. Alvaro Huerta

My brother Noel has passed away! Long live Noel!

On August 20, 2017, my brother Noel "Nene" Huerta passed away in his sleep. While uncertainty remains on the cause of death, we do know that he died suddenly and unexpectedly. He was only forty-five years old—too young to die. One day he's here, the next day he's not. While he was beloved by his family and friends—where he had his fair share of girlfriends and "flings"—he never had the opportunity to marry and have kids. Life can be cruel that way.

Noel was handsome, smart, talented and kind. He was also sensitive, gentle and generous. As a free spirit, he was one of finest human beings that I've had the honor of knowing. He made me a better person.

He was born on December 28, 1971, in Los Angeles, California. He was the seventh of eight children to Carmen Mejia Huerta and Salomon Chavez Huerta. At the time of Noel's birth, we lived with our cousins, uncles, aunts and friends in a three-story Craftsman house, located in Hollywood. Without exaggeration, as a beautiful baby and kid, he was loved by most people who got to know him at a personal level.

Despite being more like my/our mother in his sensitive demeanor, Noel also possessed the toughness of my/our father. Once we moved into the notorious Ramona Gardens housing project (or Big Hazard projects), as a kid, Noel had no choice but to adapt to the mean streets of East Los Angeles. Still, he never allowed his violent neighborhood or upbringing to vanquish his kind spirit.

In a neighborhood plagued by poverty, gangs, drugs, violence, police abuse and government neglect, Noel excelled at sports, dance, music, school and much more. When he played basketball, he was the point guard. When he played baseball, he was the pitcher. When he played football, he was the quarterback. His talent had no limits.

Given his natural talent for dance and music, he mastered pop-locking and break-dancing. As a kid, he competed with other kids throughout the city and usually prevailed by performing the windmill or spinning on his head. In his early teens, as a young DJ, he learned how to spin records on turntables during late-night, back-yard house parties.

Classified as highly gifted at an early age, he breezed through Murchison Elementary School, El Sereno Middle School and Woodrow Wilson High School. Thanks to his strong academic abilities, he was accepted to Upward Bound at Occidental College (OXY), where he spent his summer breaks to prepare for the university—something foreign to most teens from the projects. He was then admitted to UC Berkeley (UCB) and UC Santa Barbara (UCSB), where he selected the latter.

Once enrolled at UCSB, as a freshman, he became a student activist. He quickly transformed from a Chicano kid from the projects to a Chicano student activist at the university. He read every book that I gave him, from the *Autobiography of Malcolm X* to *Blood in My Eye* by George Jackson to *Occupied America: A History of Chicanos* by Dr. Rodolfo Acuña. I still have letters that Noel—as a passionate, young Chicano who wanted to change the world—wrote to me during his university years.

While Noel experienced and witnessed violent events in the projects, in Santa Barbara, nothing could prepare him for the tragic and mysterious death (near the campus) of one of his best friends, Oscar "El Bandido" Gomez, in 1994. While we'll never know what happened to Oscar—another handsome, talented and smart Chicano—this tragic incident had a major emotional and mental impact on Noel for the rest of his life.

After leaving Santa Barbara, Noel withdrew from activism, mainly due to the death of his homeboy. (Noel later earned his BA from California State University, Los Angeles). Overall, he lived a simple, non-materialistic life. He mostly spent his time with his family and friends, where he greeted everyone with a smile and hug.

Noel laughed at people's jokes, even when they were not funny. He was honest, friendly and easy-going. He didn't like too much drama or *chisme*.

It bothered Noel when people spoke negatively about him or falsely accused him of something that he didn't do or something he didn't have knowledge of. When my brother felt hurt by what people said about him—so-called "friends" and strangers—I often told him to not worry too much about what stupid and cowardly people said. I also reminded him that we—his family and friends—had his back. Nobody was going to mess with him!

Like my/our mother, he was sensitive. However, when someone tried to physically assault him or threaten his family and friends, he was the first one ready to fight. I could go on and on about my brother and all of the other great traits about him, like his sense of humor and honesty. Sometimes, he was too honest for his own good.

Yet, more than writing these humble words to honor my beloved brother, I will always regret that I didn't see him the day before he died to give him a warm hug and say, "I love you, Nene!"

FORTY-TWO

Trump Epitomizes America's History of Anti-Mexicanism

Dr. Alvaro Huerta

President Donald J. Trump represents an existential threat to Mexican immigrants and their descendants. Trump's xenophobic rhetoric and inhumane policies consist of racist, enforcement-only and divisive (e.g., "us-versus-them") positions. His domestic positions on immigration interconnect with his foreign diplomacy based on isolationism and unilateralism. While former White House administrations espoused similar anti-immigrant rhetoric and inhumane policies, such as the Chinese Exclusion Act of 1882 and the internment of an estimated 120,000 Japanese immigrants and Japanese Americans during WWII, Trump, during his short presidency, aims to re-imagine or re-invent the country's dark past with his racist slogan, "Make America Great Again." While Trump originally claimed that he coined this slogan, he actually hijacked it from the late President Ronald Reagan.

Trump, or the "Hustler-in-Chief," lies so much, it must be difficult for him—along with his lackey apologists and fellow liars, like Mike Pence, John F. Kelly, Rudy Giuliani, Kellyanne Conway, Sarah Huckabee Sanders, etc.—to keep track of all of his lies. I just hope that the brave comedian Michelle Wolf returns to the White House Correspondent's dinner, so she can ridicule and rip into Giuliani in the same manner as she exposed Sanders' infinite lies at the 2018 event.

Americans and people around the world shouldn't be surprised by Trump's serial lies, xenophobic rhetoric and racist policies. On June 16, 2015, for instance, when he delivered his infamous presidential announcement speech, Trump launched into a racist diatribe against Mexicans. In this xenophobic speech, with his immigrant wife by his side, Trump clearly connected with a significant segment of white Americans who are already receptive to anti-Mexicanism. In his brilliant essay—included in this collection of short essays (and short stories)—Dr. Juan Gómez-Quiñones posits that "U.S. anti-Mexicanism is a race premised set of historical and contemporary ascriptions, convictions and discriminatory practices inflicted on persons of Mexican descent, longstanding and pervasive in the United States . . . "

While America's brutal history of racism against African Americans is highly documented and well known, like slavery, Jim Crow and police abuse, public knowledge of racist policies against individuals of Mexican heritage—immigrants, residents and citizens—remains desperately lacking. In addition to the imperialist U.S. war against Mexico during 1846 to 1848—where Mexico lost half of its territory—the U.S. government has implemented (to the present) racist campaigns and policies against Mexican immigrants and Chicanas/os (Mexican Americans).

As part of the many draconian and inhumane cases against Mexicans in *el norte* during the twentieth century, this includes two mass deportation campaigns of this historically marginalized group: (1) "Mexican Repatriation" during the 1930s; and (2) "Operation Wetback" during the 1950s. In their insightful book, *Decade of Betrayal: Mexican Repatriation in the 1930s*, Dr. Francisco E. Balderrama and Mr. Raymond Rodríguez document that an estimated one million individuals of Mexican heritage were deported during the Great Depression, where an estimated 60 percent consisted of U.S. citizens. Regarding "Operation Wetback," then-President Dwight D. Eisenhower also ordered the deportation of over one million individuals of Mexican heritage—immigrants, residents and citizens.

Inspired by Eisenhower, during his presidential campaign, Trump praised the racist "Operation Wetback" deportation campaign. By doing so, then-candidate Trump sent a clear signal to his white nativist base, where his anti-immigration proposals and inhumane policies consist of enforcement-only measures, such as deporting millions of Mexican immigrants and building a sh*thole border wall. The underlying foundation of Trump's mass deportation fantasies (of the past) and policies (of the present) center on the eugenics ideology (or pseudo-science) dating back to the late 1800s. Coined by Francis Galton, this pseudo-science is based on the premise that to "advance" the human "race," individuals with "good" traits/genes or so-called "desirable" traits/genes (i.e., "whites") should reproduce with each other. This is why the browning of America represents a threat to the leaders and believers of this racist pseudo-science and ideology/movement.

Throughout history, the eugenics ideology/movement has been used by racist individuals and groups, like the Nazis in Germany and bigots in the United States, to claim that the Aryan "race" is genetically superior compared to other "races" or racialized groups. Prior to the rise of Nazism, white Americans used this pseudo-science to argue that they were superior to African Americans, Mexican Americans, Native Americans and Asian Americans. For instance, as a way to justify their racist policies against African Americans throughout American history, like slavery and Jim Crow, white American leaders and white citizens claimed (to the present) that whites were/are superior to African Americans.

In his *Los Angeles Times'* op-ed, the award-winning writer Michael D'Antonio, focusing on the plight of undocumented youth, connects Trump's decision to end DACA (Deferred Action for Childhood Arrivals), which provides temporary deportation relief and work permits for many undocumented youth, to eugenics: "There is another distinction that sets Dreamers apart, of course: Most of them are from Mexico, and they are not white. Trump's move to end DACA, therefore, must be understood within the historical context of America's exclusionary immigration policies, the bulk of which have relied on the pseudoscience of eugenics."

As a divisive leader, Trump has played his "us-versus-them" card from his presidential campaign to his presidency. Be it Mexican immigrants, Muslim Americans or African American athletes (e.g., athletes who refuse to stand for the American flag due to rampant police abuse), Trump represents the next "great-white-hope" to protect white Americans, especially the working-class, against the so-called "brown barbarians at the gate." Hence, Trump's fetish or fantasy for a southern border wall, which Mexico will "miraculously" pay for, makes absolute sense. Instead of focusing on bridges that unite us, Trump is focusing on walls that divide us. In his superb book, *Why Walls Won't Work: Repairing the US-Mexico Divide*, Dr. Michael Dear of UC Berkeley brilliantly makes the case that walls don't work. By analyzing history, he also argues that walls eventually come down.

While Trump has solidified his racist credentials, there's no denying that a large share of American voters—the almost 63 million citizens who voted for him—bought his racist message. Actually, it's not that Trump convinced them to be racist—they're racist to begin with. For example, how many of them abandoned Trump when he disparaged immigrants from El Salvador, Haiti and African countries during a White House-led meeting on January 11, 2018? At this official meeting, Trump reportedly said, "Why are we having all these people from shithole countries come here?" (*The Washington Post*, January 12, 2018). To remove any doubt of his racist credentials, Trump also inquired about bringing more immigrants from European countries, like Norway.

By examining Trump's domestic immigration policies, we can better understand his foreign positions and their negative consequences. If Trump insists on building a stupid border wall, for instance, does this create an incentive for Mexico—as a friendly neighbor and major trading partner—to aggressively pursue alternative trading partners, like China, Russia and the European Union (EU)?

While Mexican President Enrique Peña Nieto and his ruling party— PRI or *Partido Revolucionario Institucional*—constantly cave or bow to Trump, there's no guarantee that the leading 2018 presidential candidate, Andrés Manuel López Obrador (AMLO), will continue to capitulate to Trump and *los gringos*.

While the U.S. remains a superpower with asymmetric diplomatic relations throughout world, its leaders—Trump and the morally bank- rupt Republican Party—and its citizens, especially Trump's white work- ing-class supporters, must decide if they want to use their enormous military and economic power for good or evil? Unless Trump gets im- peached, where his entire administration must resign, especially the equally dangerous Vice President Mike Pence, a significant segment of the world—especially the marginalized and oppressed—will continue to perceive the American citizen via a singular gaze: "the Ugly American."

FORTY-THREE

A Call for Urban Planning Latina/o Faculty

In Memory of Dr. Leo Estrada

Dr. Alvaro Huerta

On November 3, 2018, the urban planning community in general and Latina/o community in particular experienced a devastating blow with the death of Dr. Leo Estrada. As one of the few Latina/o urban planning faculty members in the country, Dr. Estrada (or Leo, which he preferred) was a pioneer for planning scholars (and practitioners). Originally from Texas, he obtained a tenure-track, faculty position at UCLA's Department of Urban Planning in 1977. He held this faculty position until his retirement, as an associate professor, in June of 2018.

Leo represented the best academe and humanity have to offer. He was brilliant, articulate, confident, open-minded, humorous, kind, approachable, generous, community focused, family oriented, visionary and strategic. He was a mentor and guide, a trailblazer and pioneer, a leader and producer of leaders. Overall, he was an amazing human being.

While I'm not sure if he's the first Latina/o to secure a tenure-track, faculty position in urban planning, I can say that, during the past forty years, few Latinas/os have become tenure-track or tenured faculty members in urban planning departments throughout this country. I should know, because I am one of them. As a faculty member, I'm most concerned that Latina/o faculty members and students, especially Chicanas/os (Mexican Americans) from historically marginalized communities, who have been excluded from institutions of higher education, particularly elite colleges/universities.

In a country where more than 57.5 million citizens/residents are Latinas/os, not including the over three million Puerto Ricans on the island, who are U.S. citizens, it's a shame that an important field like urban planning has so few Latina/o faculty members. We need many more faculty members like Leo, who can teach, advice and mentor the next generation of Latina/o planners in all sectors of society, including government, private industry and nonprofit sector.

During the early 2000s, when I first applied to the master's program at UCLA's Department of Urban Planning, I didn't know much about the field. Having spent thirteen years as a community organizer, I was out of the loop in terms of graduate school, despite earning my BA in History from UCLA.

"Talk to Leo, before you apply," my old undergraduate contacts encouraged me. Actually, it was more like a collective mandate: "If you want to get accepted, go see Leo!"

I kept saying to myself, "Who is this Leo guy?" So, I started to visit the campus and wandered around the Public Affairs Building, where Leo's office was located, hoping to "accidentally" bump into him. On second thought, I acted more like a groupie of a famous singer, like Bono from the rock band U2.

Two months later, after my master plan failed, I finally mustered up the courage to email Leo, asking for a one-on-one meeting to learn more about the program. Five minutes later, he responded, "Absolutely. I've been waiting for you." The rest is history.

To me, he represented the Latino version of the Oracle—the wise African American woman with the power of foresight—from the movie *The Matrix* (1999), starring Keanu Reeves as Neo. Does that make me the Chicano version of Neo? (Actually, I'm better-looking than Keanu.)

Once I was accepted into the program, I quickly learned the importance of having a faculty member, at the graduate level, who looked like me. (Actually, he was better-looking than me.) As one of the few Latina/o graduate students from a working-class background and violent barrio at an elite university, I especially appreciated having someone who was sympathetic to my harsh upbringing.

I was born to Mexican immigrant parents without formal education and grew up on the mean streets of East Los Angeles. That put me at a disadvantage with my privileged classmates, when I originally entered UCLA (as a seventeen-year-old freshman, majoring in mathematics). Even among the few Latina/o students on campus, I was an outlier. Consequently, as an undergraduate, I relied on Dr. Juan Gómez-Quiñones— one of the few Chicana/o faculty members—to succeed.

During graduate school, Leo played a similar role to Dr. Gómez-Quiñones. While he wasn't my assigned adviser, he never closed his door to me or other students who sought his guidance. Whenever I ran into an obstacle with another faculty member or grappled with a complex research question, I could always count on him. As we would say in my old barrio, "My homeboy Leo always had my back."

Because of Leo—and my wise wife, Antonia, and late mother, Carmen—I am the only Chicana/o in the country to earn combined urban planning degrees from UCLA (MA) and UC Berkeley (PhD). This has allowed me to secure a faculty position. This has also allowed me to write books, peer-reviewed articles and deliver lectures throughout the world.

As a faculty member, like Leo's tenure at UCLA, I'm in a privileged position to teach, advise and mentor the next generation of Latinas/os in the planning field and beyond, where these amazing students—many of them first-generation university students—assume leadership roles in society and become role models in their communities, once they graduate. While many professors disdain service-related duties, like advising and mentoring, taking them away from their research projects and professional goals, I embrace such duties, as part of my academic duties. When asked about my commitment to service, which applies to my brilliant colleague and good friend Leo, I usually cite the acclaimed singer Lady Gaga: "Baby, I was born this way."

Following in the footsteps of Leo, I have a moral obligation to teach, advise and mentor students, particularly those with similar traits and experiences like mine: first-generation Latinas/os students raised in the barrio, children of immigrants and students of working-class backgrounds. Such efforts are vital so that they, too, can secure advanced degrees from elite universities to serve the less fortunate among us.

That brings me to my persistent call for more urban planning departments in particular—and, in fact, many more academic departments in general—to recruit, train and hire more tenure-track, Latina/o faculty members. And they should place a particular emphasis on Chicanas/os, given that Chicanas/os represent the largest subgroup of Latinas/os in this country.

In short, higher education definitely needs a lot more faculty like Leo. *¡Viva el gran maestro y ser humano Leo Estrada!*

FORTY-FOUR

I Am Not Your "Wetback"

Dr. Alvaro Huerta

To paraphrase the great American writer James Baldwin, I declare to America's racists that I am not your "wetback." I am a man. I am a Chicano. I am a proud son of Mexican immigrants—the salt of the earth.

I say these words from a place of privilege with my university degrees and academic status. I also say these words based on my personal and familial background plagued by abject poverty, violence and, overall, sense of hopelessness. This includes spending the first four years of my life in a Mexican *colonia* (Colonia Libertad, Tijuana, Baja California) and formative years in a violent American barrio (East Los Angeles, California).

When I say that I am not your "wetback," it doesn't just apply to myself. It also applies to the millions of resilient and proud people of Mexican origin in this country. By studying history, we learn about the deep roots or ties that Mexicans have to this land, preceding the *gringo* settlers/invaders with their bloody annexations of Mexico's territory (an estimated 50 percent)—starting with Texas in 1836 and the remaining half by 1848. That's almost 200 years of state violence, psychological punishment, humiliation and exploitation against Mexicans immigrants and Chicana/os (Mexican Americans)—*mi gente*.

Yet, some might argue that I don't speak for the 35.8 million people of Mexican heritage in this country. While I don't speak on behalf of all Mexicans in *el norte*, especially the Latina/o Trump supporters who ventured into the dark side, I must say that I feel morally compelled to defend this historically disenfranchised and racialized group. I feel this way since I see a lack of strong leadership, on a national level, by Latina/o elected officials, organizational leaders and scholars to directly challenge, without apologies, the scapegoating of brown people for America's woes.

White elitists, like Trump, have successfully convinced millions of white working-class individuals/families that they lack social, educational and financial mobility because "the Mexicans" are "invading their country," "overburdening" public schools and "stealing" American jobs. When this occurs, we need more Latina/o leaders to respond with strength and conviction.

In attempting to distance themselves from Trump's racist argument or frame, many so-called Latina/o leaders often respond by saying, "We are not all invaders, criminals, social burdens and job thieves." By doing so, as the distinguished linguist Dr. George Lakoff argues in his excellent book, *The All New Don't Think of an Elephant!:Know Your Values and Frame the Debate,* this only reinforces Trump's racist frame. "Frames," Lakoff argues, "are mental structures that shape the way we see the world" (xxi). We must be careful in how we respond when refuting frames with the frame's same language or terminology, as Lakoff posits: "When you argue against someone on the other side using their language and their frames, you are activating their frames, strengthening their frames in those who hear you, and undermining your own views" (xii). Thus, instead of accepting the premise of Trump's racist frames about Mexicans, along with his deplorable supporters, we must reject their premises without giving it any credence to them. This doesn't imply that we don't respond. On the contrary, we do so without apologies!

Unfortunately, in trying to be accepted by the dominant culture, too many of these so-called Latina/o leaders and many average Latinas/os will say something like, "I am an American; not a 'criminal' or an 'illegal.'" Again, this type of language or terminology only reinforces the racist frame(s) perpetuated against brown people by Trump and fellow bigots—who hold similar views, yet, have refined their use of language, like the oleaginous Vice President Mike Pence. (I borrowed the esoteric term "oleaginous" from the conservative writer George F. Will to describe the greasy Pence.)

It's long overdue for Chicanas/os and Mexican immigrants to unite and reject all racist rhetoric, actions and policies by American leaders and millions of white citizens against our people. To do so, we must be proud of our ethnic roots and speak out against all forms of discrimination in public and private spheres. We must also reject all false labels, categories and typologies that divide us: working-class versus middle-class; educated versus uneducated; citizen versus undocumented; undocumented youth ("good immigrants" or "the innocent ones") versus undocumented parents ("bad immigrants" or "the sinners"), etc.

Moreover, we must recognize that we come from a proud people with a rich history, where we don't need to be apologetic or embarrassed of our indigenous roots and socio-economic status—past and present.

I must admit that, as a teenager, I was embarrassed of my Mexican immigrant parents on at least two occasions. On one occasion, at the age of thirteen, my father decided to take my brother Salomon—now a critically acclaimed artist—and me to Malibu, California, to work as day laborers. Originally, it was my mother's idea to ensure that we did well in school by experiencing the hardships of manual labor. (In fact, many Mexican immigrant parents share a similar life lesson with their lazy American-raised kids/teens when they tell them: "I want you to do well in school so you don't suffer like me!) After a two-hour bus ride from the Eastside to the Westside, we found ourselves on a freezing street corner, where I witnessed my father chasing luxury cars and "begging" the rich white drivers to work on their beachfront lawns. Seeing my father "run and beg" for work, I wanted to run toward the ocean from sheer embarrassment. (Luckily for me, I didn't know how to swim.)

On another occasion, at the age of seventeen, I was attending UCLA's Freshman Summer Program (FSP)—as one of few Chicanas/os from a working-class background to attend this elite university in 1985. On the first day of class, during introductions, while my mostly privileged classmates boasted about their educated and professional parents, I immediately felt embarrassed of my mother's status (domestic worker) and father's status (unemployed). It didn't help that we lived in public housing projects (with subsided rent) and depended on government aid. This included monetary aid, free school meals, "Reagan cheese," Medical and food stamps. Speaking of food stamps, while growing up, we operated with fake money (i.e., booklet of food stamps), as if living in a real-life Monopoly board game.

It wasn't until I became a student activist as a member of MEChA (*Movimiento Estudiantil Chicana/o de Aztlán*) and majored in history (changed from mathematics)—when I learned the true history of my people and studied the inherent contradictions of American capitalism—that I became proud of my Mexican parents and working-class roots. I owe this to the teachings of several Chicana/o scholars, along with my independent research on Marxism and other fields, advancing my understanding (past and present) of the Mexican people on both sides of the border.

Moving forward, Chicanas/os and Mexicans must be fearless, learning from our long history of resistance, from the Aztec battles against the bloody *conquistador* Hernán Cortés (and his savage men) to the Chicana/o Movement of the 1960s/1970s to the Latino gardeners grassroots campaign against a draconian city law in the late 1990s to the brave undocumented youth of the present. We must also live and work without seeking validation from the dominant society. Moreover, we must always walk with our heads held high, demanding to be treated with dignity and respect.

Conclusion

Dr. Alvaro Huerta

In writing these short essays and stories during the past decade, I've consistently challenged the scapegoating of brown people by American leaders (mostly conservatives), conservative media outlets (e.g., Fox News) and millions of citizens for this country's woes. In doing so, my aim has been to reframe the debate over Latina/o immigrants in particular and Latinas/os in general, where we should treat Latina/o immigrants and their offspring with dignity and respect. Given that I don't compromise when it comes to the human rights of honest people on the move, I've also sought to set an example for others—particularly those who believe in equality and justice for all—on how to stand firm and be vocal, without apologies, on behalf of those who live and work in America's shadows.

Speaking of standing firm and being vocal, Democratic leaders in Congress have finally found their mojo against President Donald J. Trump. As of January 21, 2019, for instance, the United States government remains partially shutdown for one month due to Trump's childish behavior for demanding $5.7 billion to build his racist border wall, where Democrats have remained united against appropriating funds for the wall.

Throughout the ongoing debate over the government shutdown, border security and the wall, Trump suffers from selective amnesia: he conveniently "forgets" what doesn't benefit him and only "remembers" what's in his best interest. While Trump took full credit for a potential government shutdown on December 11, 2018, in an official meeting with Speaker of the House Nancy Pelosi and Senate Minority Leader Chuck Schumer, for instance, he keeps blaming Democrats for the shutdown.

Also, he conveniently "forgets" that he promised the American public and his deplorable supporters during his presidential campaign, especially at his neo-Nazi simulated rallies, that Mexico would "miraculously" pay for his fantasy wall. Now that Mexico hasn't transferred the billions of *pesos* to the U.S. government to build his stupid wall, especially with the new leadership under President Andrés Manuel López Obrador (AMLO), Trump wants the American tax-payers to build his medieval "solution" to a twenty-first century problem.

173

As part of his failed plan to partially shutdown the government to secure his $5.7 billion ransom from Congress for his promised wall—which he keeps changes the type of material, from concrete to fence to steel to "peaches" (CNN, January 11, 2019)—Trump, along with his immoral surrogates, like Mike Pence, Sarah Huckabee Sanders, Kellyanne Conway, Mick Mulvaney and Kirstjen Nielsen, keeps lying about the so-called emergency at the border. While border crossings by undocumented immigrants have been declining over the years, according to the *New York Times* (June 20, 2018) and other media sources, Trump and fellow liars erroneously claim that the country is experiencing a "crises" at the southern border. In fact, according to reporter Timothy Noah of POLITICO (November 2, 2018), border arrests in 2017 had dropped so low that "to find a year with fewer border arrests, you have to go back all the way to 1971." From 1971 to 2017, that's almost fifty years!

Speaking of lies, Trump and his cronies keep repeating other lies about the so-called border emergency and need for a wall for which Mexico will never pay for. This includes the outrageous lie or stupid notion that terrorists, like ISIS, are crossing the southern border by the thousands! Does the average Trump supporter actually believe that Mexico, as a Catholic-dominated country with an effective police state, will allow Muslim terrorists to establish military bases or networks on its soil? I'll bet any Trump supporter 10,000 *pesos* that if the Mexican government won't capture and kill these "imaginary terrorists," the drug cartels and gangs will. Putting religion and national pride aside, ISIS is bad for business for drug cartels and gangs! For any criminal enterprise, just like the U.S. invasion and occupation of Iraq, along with the government's illegal interference in Venezuela's domestic issues, it's all about claiming and controlling territory!

There are so many lies spewed from Trump's mouth that it's difficult to keep up with, like the lie that 90 percent of heroine entering the country comes from the southern border. While some drugs do come from the southern border, like in the case of tunnels, which a wall doesn't stop, the majority come from legal ports of entry, according to *USA Today* (January 16, 2019) and other reliable sources.

In terms of drugs, let's not forget the major domestic players in today's drug crisis, such as pharmaceutical companies, lobbyists and complicit doctors who have flooded the market with overprescribed drugs which are consumed by the American public. Many of these drugs are also illegally sold, traded and exchanged in the informal economy! This also includes to the major television networks where virtually every other commercial is paid by a pharmaceutical company, peddling drugs. Moreover, I find it ironic that suddenly we're all aware and worried about the drug crisis, like the opioid crisis or opioid epidemic, once it primarily hits white people in cities, suburbs and rural communities. Where were all of the same American leaders, policy makers and concerned citizens when drugs (and alcohol) were disproportionately impacting Latinas/os and African Americans in America's inner-cities during the 1980s and 1990s? How about the long drug crisis impacting Native American's in reservations?

Ultimately, the important issue about the partial government shutdown is not really about the border wall. It's more about the current wave of white supremacy and white nativism that America is experiencing, as epitomized by the election of Trump. Essentially, for millions of white people in this country, they can't accept we're going through major demographic changes with the browning of America. (To be fair and objective, there are millions of white Americans who reject racism and embrace diversity.) Thus, it's incumbent on all of us who reject racism and embrace diversity to stand up and speak out against bigotry in all its shapes and colors, as illustrated by the "Orange-Man-in-the-White House."

Works Cited

Acuña, Rudolfo. *Occupied America: A History of Chicanos*. Fifth Edition. Pearson Longman, 2004.

"AICP Code of Ethics and Professional Conduct." American Planning Association, Revised 1 April 2016, https://www.planning.org/ethics/ethicscode/. Accessed 1 July 2016.

Anderson, Bridget. "Imagining a World Without Border." *YouTube*, uploaded by TEDx Talks, 22 Sept. 2011, https://www.youtube.com/watch?v=zht-6BrX1b4.

Anzaldúa, Gloria. *Borderland / La Frontera: The New Mestiza*. Spinsters / Aunt Lute, 1987.

Balderrama, Francisco E. and Raymond Rodríguez. *Decade of Betrayal: Mexican Repatriation in the 1930s*. Revised Edition. University of New Mexico Press, 2006.

Burke, Daniel. "Pope suggests Trump 'is not Christian'." CNN, 18 Feb. 2016, https://www.cnn.com/2016/02/18/politics/pope-francis-trump-christian-wall/index.html. Accessed 20 Feb. 2016.

Chemerinsky, Erwin, Annie Lai and Seth Davis. "Trump Can't Force 'Sanctuary Cities' to Enforce his Deportation Plans." *The Washington Post*, 22. Dec. 22, 2016, https://www.washingtonpost.com/opinions/trump-cant-force-sanctuary-cities-to-enforce-his-deportation-plans/2016/12/22/421174d4-c7a4-11e6-85b5-76616a33048d_story.html?utm_term=.ff04fa085a08. Accessed 25 Dec. 2016.

Cornelius, Wayne A., Angela S. García and Monica W. Varsanyi. "Giving sanctuary to Undocumented Immigrants Doesn't Threaten Public Safety—It Increases It." *Los Angeles Times*, 2 Feb. 2017, https://www.latimes.com/opinion/op-ed/la-oe-sanctuary-cities-trump-20170202-story.html. Accessed 5 Feb. 2017.

Eder, Steve and Dave Phillips. "Donald Trump's Draft Deferments: Four for College, One for Bad Feet." *New York Times* , 1 Aug. 2016, https://www.nytimes.com/2016/08/02/us/politics/donald-trump-draft-record.html. Accessed 5 Sept. 2016.

D'Antonio, Michael. Trump's Move to End DACA has Roots in America's Long, Shameful History of Eugenics." *Los Angeles Times*, 14 Sept. 2017, https://www.latimes.com/opinion/op-ed/la-oe-antonio-trump-eugenics-daca-20170914-story.html. Accessed 5 May 2018.

Dawsey, John. "Trump Derides Protections for Immigrants from 'Shithole' Countries." *The Washington Post*, 12 Jan. 2018, https://www.washingtonpost.com/politics/trump-attacks-protections-for-immigrants-from-shithole-countries-in-oval-office-meeting/2018/01/11/bfc0725c-f711-11e7-91af-31ac729add94_story.html?utm_term=.bf0a0266c2d6. Accessed 14 Jan. 2018.

Dear, Michael. *Why Walls Won't Work: Repairing the U.S.-Mexico Divide*. Oxford UP, 2013.

———. "Mr. President, Tear Down This Wall." *The New York Times*, 10 March 2013, https://www.nytimes.com/2013/03/11/opinion/mr-president-tear-down-this-wall.html. Accessed 22 Jan. 2018.

Dreier, Peter. "What Housing Recovery?" *New York Times*, 8 May 2014, https://www.nytimes.com/2014/05/09/opinion/what-housing-recovery.html. Accessed 9 May 2014.

Dreyfuss, Ben. "No, Megyn Kelly, Santa Is Not White." *Mother Jones*, 12 Dec. 2013, https://www.motherjones.com/politics/2013/12/megyn-kelly-jesus-santa-black-white/. Accessed 14 Dec. 2013.

Felbab-Brown, Vanda. "Trump's Counterproductive Attacks on Sanctuary Cities." Brookings, 31 Jan. 2017. https://www.brookings.edu/blog/order-from-chaos/2017/01/31/trumps-counterproductive-attack-on-sanctuary-cities/. Accessed 1 Feb. 2017.

Freire, Paulo. *Pedagogy of the Oppressed.* 30th Anniversary Edition. The Continuum International Publishing Group, Inc., 2000.

Gomez, Anthony. " Fact-checking Trump Officials: Most Drugs Enter US through Legal Ports of Entry, not Vast, Open Border." *USA Today*, 16 Jan. 2019. https://www.usatoday.com/story/news/politics/2019/01/16/fact-check-mike-pence-donald-trump-drugs-crossing-southern-border-wall/2591279002/. Accessed 18 Jan. 2019.

Gonzales, Manuel G. *Mexicanos: A History of Mexicans in the United States.* Second Edition. Indiana UP, 2009.

Hiltzik, Michael. "All the Horrific Details of the GOP's New Obamacare Repeal Bill: A handy Guide." *Los Angeles Times.* 5 May 2017, https://www.latimes.com/business/hiltzik/la-fi-hiltzik-obamacare-repeal-20170504-story.html. Accessed 6 May 2017.

Huerta, Alvaro. "Migration as a Universal Human Right." *YouTube*, uploaded by TEDx Talks, 21 July 2015, https://www.youtube.com/watch?v=17fi3buAscY.

———. *Reframing the Latino Immigration Debate: Towards a Humanistic Paradigm.* San Diego State UP, 2013.

———. "Examining the Perils and Promises of an Informal Niche in a Global City: A Case Study of Mexican Immigrant Gardeners in Los Angeles." PhD diss., University of California, Berkeley, 2011.

———. "Looking Beyond 'Mow, Blow and Go': Mexican Immigrant Gardeners in Los Angeles. *Berkeley Planning Journal*, vol. 20, 2007, pp. 1 - 23.

———. "The Answer is Blowin' in the Wind: A Case Study of Latino Gardeners Organizing in Los Angeles." Master's thesis, University of California, Los Angeles, 2006.

———. "South Gate, California: Environmental Racism Defeated in Blue-Collar Latino Suburb." *Critical Planning*, vol. 12, 2005, pp. 92–102.

Huerta, Alvaro and Alfonso Morales. "The Formation of a Grassroots Movement: The Association of Latin American Gardeners of Los Angeles Challenges City Hall." *Aztlán : A Journal of Chicano Studies*, vol. 39, no. 2, 2014, pp. 65–93.

Huntington, Samuel P. "The Hispanic Challenge." *Foreign Affairs*, 28 Oct. 2009, http://foreignpolicy.com/2009/10/28/the-hispanic-challenge/. Accessed 8 July 2017.

Hyman, Louis and Natasha Islander. "What the Mass Deportation of Immigrants Might Look Like." *Slate*, 16 Nov. 2016. http://www.slate.com/articles/news_and_politics/history/2016/11/donald_trump_mass_deportation_and_the_tragic_history_of_operation_wetback.html. (Accessed 3 July 2017)

Lakoff, George. *The ALL NEW Don't Think of an Elephant!: Know Your Values and Frame the Debate.* Chelsea Green Publishing, 2014.

Lee, Michelle Ye Hee. "Donald Trump's False Comments Connecting Mexican Immigrants and Crime." *The Washington Post*, 8 July 2015, https://www.washingtonpost.com/news/fact-checker/wp/2015/07/08/donald-trumps-false-comments-connecting-mexican-immigrants-and-crime/?utm_term=.769dd9e5b852. Accessed 9 July 2015.

Liu, Yvonne Yen, Patrick Burns and Daniel Flaming. *Sidewalk Stimulus: Economic and Geographic Impact of Los Angeles Street Vendors.* Economic Roundtable, 2015.

Magón, Ricardo Flores. "Carta a Nicolás Bernal." 30 de Octobre de 1920. *Sembradores Ricardo Flores Magón Y El Partido Liberal Mexicano: A Eulogy and Critique.* Juan Gómez-Quiñones. Aztlan Publications, Chicano Studies Center, 1973, 140–141.

Martinez, Nancy. "Ruben Salazar Remembered." EGP News, 4 Sept. 2014, http://egpnews.com/2014/09/ruben-salazar-remembered/. Accessed 1 Aug. 2017.

McGonigal, Jane. "Gaming and Productivity." *YouTube*, uploaded by Big Think, 3 July 2012, www.youtube.com/watch?v=mkdzy9bWW3E.

Noah, Timothy. " Immigration Crisis? The Stats Tell a Different Story." POLITICO, 11 Feb. 2018, https://www.politico.com/story/2018/11/02/immigration-crisis-fact-check-916924 Accessed 22 June 2018.

"Panel: 'Organizing Latino Immigrants in the Informal Economy.'" *YouTube*, uploaded by UCLA Chicano Studies Research Center, 13 May 2015, https://www.youtube.com/watch?v=Bq4ZQlpm-_k.

Parker, Ashley, Josh Dawsey and Ed O'Keefe. "'Negotiating with Jell-O': How Trump's Shifting Positions Fueled the Rush to a Shutdown." *The Washington Post*, 20 Jan. 2018, https://www.washingtonpost.com/politics/negotiating-with-jell-o-how-trumps-shifting-positions-fueled-the-rush-to-a-shutdown/2018/01/20/81215b90-fd71-11e7-a46b-a3614530bd87_story.html?utm_term=.a6b7e991e8c6. Accessed 22 Jan. 2018.

Parlapiano, Alicia and Anjali Singhvi. "The Supreme Court Partially Allowed Trump's Travel Ban. Who Is Still Barred?" *New York Times*, 29 June 2017, https://www.nytimes.com/interactive/2017/06/29/us/politics/supreme-court-trump-travel-ban.html. (Accessed 6 July 2017)

Qui, Linda. "Border Crossings Have Been Declining for Years, Despite Claims of a 'Crisis of Illegal Immigration.'" *New York Times*, 20 June 2018, https://www.nytimes.com/2018/06/20/us/politics/fact-check-trump-border-crossings-declining-.html. Accessed 22 June 2018.

Schwartz, Ian, "Trump: 'Latinos Love Trump and I Love Them." Real Clear Politics, 23 June 2015, https://www.realclearpolitics.com/video/2015/06/23/trump_latinos_love_trump_and_i_love_them.html. Accessed 24 June 2015.

Senate Bill 54. Author Senator De León. State of California. http://leginfo.legislature.ca.gov/faces/billNavClient.xhtml?bill_id=201720180SB54

Takaki, Ronald. *A Different Mirror: A History of Multicultural America*. Back Bay Books / Little, Brown and Company, 2008.

Unz, Ron. "His-Panic: The Myth of Immigrant Crime." *The American Conservative*, March 2010, http://www.unz.com/wp-content/uploads/2015/07/HispanicCrime.pdf. Accessed 24 Aug. 2017.

Zurcher, Anthony. "Five reasons Trump Still Tops the Polls." BBC News, 27 July 2015, https://www.bbc.com/news/world-us-canada-33660969. Accessed 28 July 2015.

Index

Monty, Jacob, 111
Movimiento Estudiantil Chicano de Aztlán. See MEChA
Mt. Gleason Jr. High School: classism at, 20; faculty racism at, 20; identity categories and, 24; student racism at, 19–20
Mueller, Robert, 149
Murchison Elementary School, 19
Murguia, Janet, 143–144
Muslim ban, 105, 120, 122, 123; urban planning and, 106
Muslims, 122; Mexico and Muslim terrorists, 174

Nadel, Leonard, 70
NAFTA. *See* North American Free Trade Agreement
National Council of La Raza (NCLR), 143
Native Americans, 89–90; colonialism and, 10–11; Indian Removal Act and, 90; Mexican American relations with, 11–12; Pequot, 10; white supremacy and, 10
nativism: anti-Mexicanism and, 9; Trump and, xvii–xviii, 83, 162
Nazis, 162–163
NCLR. *See* National Council of La Raza
neo-Nazi, 173
Nixon, Richard M., 149
el norte, 25; immigrant contributions in, 7; land loss of, 6; mass deportation campaigns in, 90, 162; Mexican immigration to, 6; Treaty of Guadalupe Hidalgo and, 6; Trump supporters in, 169
North American Free Trade Agreement (NAFTA), xvii; Trump and, 116

Obama, Barack, 41, 103; on American exceptionalism, 36; border militarization and, 47–48; "Border Security, Economic Opportunity, and Immigration Modernization Act" and, 34, 35; DACA and, 49, 93, 94; DAPA and, 93, 94; deportations by, xviii, 35–36, 37, 47, 103, 143; as

"Deporter-in-Chief," 103, 143–144; immigration executive orders (2014) of, 93, 94; Latina/o votes for, 103, 144; Murguia and, 143–144; Republican obstructionism and, 147
Obamacare. *See* Affordable Care Act
Occupied America: A History of Chicanos (Acuña), 6
"Operation Wetback," 90, 96, 122; Eisenhower and, 162
"Orange-man-in-the-White House". *See* Trump, Donald J.
organizing strategies, xviii; in social movement building, 41. *See also* community organizing

Parks, Rosa, 41
pathway to citizenship, 47; "Border Security, Economic Opportunity, and Immigration Modernization Act" and, 33, 35
Pedagogy of the Oppressed (Freire), 27
Peña Nieto, Enrique, 164
Pence, Mike, 149, 164, 170
Pequot Native Americans, 10
Perez, Alcadio, 58–59
Perez, Pedro, 28, 30
Perry, Rick, 51–52
Piketty, Thomas, 43
police abuse, 23, 55, 110; barrios and, 19, 53; in East Los Angeles, 95; justice for, 53; Latino officers and, 95; Ramona Gardens housing project and, 54–55; riots and, 53–54; at UCLA, 55
power plant, 28, 31
Proposition 187, 50

Quayle, Dan, 109

racial hierarchy, 11, 12–13; labor force and, 7
racism: classism and, 20; colonialism and, 10–11; frames of, 170; labor force and, 7; mixed heritage and, 11–12; at Mt. Gleason Jr. High School, 19–20; race and, 11–12; racial slurs, 19; Trump and, 77, 78, 81, 83, 107, 110, 122, 161–162; U.S.-

Mexico relations and, 11

Ramirez, Alfredo, 57

Ramona Gardens housing project, 54, 109; Big Hazard projects and, 17, 23, 54, 73; Chuco and Huerta, S. C., at, 62–63; fights at, 61; Huerta, N., in, 157–158; moving to, 61–62; police abuse and, 54–55

Reagan, Ronald: on Berlin Wall, 90; campaign slogan of, 102, 161; IRCA and, 94

re-frame, 3; Latino gardeners and, 141

Reframing the Latino Immigration Debate (Huerta, A.), 151

Republican Party, 94; abortion and, 113; Asian and Pacific Islander voters and, 49, 50; Boehner and, 48, 49; class warfare of, 82; comprehensive immigration reform and, 47–48; DACA and, 49; DAPA and, 48; ISIS terrorists and, 99; Latina/o voters and, 48, 49, 50, 80, 84, 94, 96; obstructionism of, 147; Trump and platform of, 81, 84; Wilson and, 50; xenophobia as and, 94

resilience, 21

reverse white flight, 40–41

Riis, Jacob, 105

El Robo, 57

Rodríguez, Raymond, 162

Romney, Mitt, 48, 78, 84; self-deportation and, 94

Roosevelt, Franklin Delano, 84

Rosa (friend), 58

Rubio, Marco, 95–96, 99; "Little Marco," 102; Trump and, 96

Ryan, Paul D., 116

Sajo Grande: family feuds in, 61, 66; Huerta, C. M., in, 57; Huerta, S. C., in, 61, 65

Salazar, Ruben, 2, 125, 129; frame and, 131–134; political interest in, 132; shooter of, 134, 135; targeting of, 132, 133

Salmon, Matt, 79–80

sanctuary cities: anti-sanctuary city legislation, 79, 80, 120; ICE and, 79;

Trump and, 120

sanctuary state, 119, 123; reasons for, 119, 120

Sanders, Bernie, 103, 161

Saturday Night Live, 89, 91

SB 1070, 141

scholar-activist, 40, 156; asymmetric spaces and, 153; publishing for, 155; rational actor and, 154; respect for, 155

Schumer, Charles E., 33, 149, 150

SEIU-USWW, 29

El Sereno Middle School, 158

Silver Dollar Bar, 134, 135

sinvergüenza, 117

slavery, 98, 163; Mexico and, 6

Smiley, Tavis, 101

social change, 12

social movement building: agitate in, 41; educate in, 40–41; organize in, 41

social networks, 29–30

Spanish *conquistadores*, 117

Steinle, Kathryn, 79–80

storytelling, 1

street vendors: benefits of, 87; decriminalizing, 86–87; at El Gallo Bakery, 85; history of, 86; informal economy and, 86; legalizing, 85–86, 87; Los Angeles Street Vendor Campaign, 86

student activism, 39; ChEP and, 73; confidence and, 73, 74; Huerta, N., as, 158; hunger strike at UCLA as, 28, 154; MEChA and, 27–28, 73; privilege and, 28–29; role of, 28

Supreme Court, 147

Takaki, Ronald, 7; on activism and organizing, 7–8; *A Different Mirror: A History of Multicultural America* by, 5, 6

temporary protected status (TPS), 147

terrorism, 107; child refugees and, 51–52; ISIS and, 99, 114, 174; Mexico and Muslim, 174

Texas, historical: Adams purchase offer for, 6; annexation of, 6; *gringos* in, 5–6, 118, 169; as homeland, 6; Mexican customs and, 5

About the Author

Alvaro Huerta, PhD, holds a joint faculty appointment in Urban & Regional Planning (URP) and Ethnic & Women's Studies (EWS) at California State Polytechnic University, Pomona. He's the author of the book *Reframing the Latino Immigration Debate: Towards a Humanistic Paradigm.* He's also the lead editor of *People of Color in the United States: Contemporary Issues in Education, Work, Communities, Health, and Immigration* (Volume 4). He earned a PhD in City and Regional Planning from UC Berkeley. He also earned an MA in Urban Planning and a BA in History from UCLA.